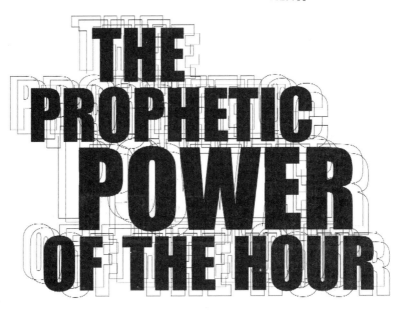

THE PROPHETIC POWER OF THE HOUR

A Revolutionary Revelation

By
Irma Elizabeth Diaz

Christian Living Books, Inc.
Largo, MD

ISBN 0-9716240-0-3

Scripture quotations unless otherwise stated,are from the King James Version of the Bible.

Irma Elizabeth Diaz
President and Founder
Upon This Rock Ministries
P. O. Box 2146
Covina, CA 91722
(888) 567-7474
www.IrmaDiaz.org

Published by Christian Living Books, Inc.
An imprint of Pneuma Life Publishing, Inc.
P. O. Box 7584
Largo, MD 20792
301-218-9092
www.ChristianLivingBooks.com
www.pneumalife.com

Printed in the United States of America

DEDICATION

I dedicate this book first to my "Abba" Father, whose Essence holds my Beloved Messiah and Bridegroom, Jesus Christ and whose heart yearns for the harmonious sound of creation seeking their Creator. It is my prayer that You are pleased, Adonai.

To Pastor Ken Clowdus, Community Christian Center and the 5:00 a.m. prayer team. Thank you for the many years you have prayed for me and my family. And, to prayer intercessors all over the world who because of your diligence have created a "Harmony of Influence" that has reached the heart of God. Thank you! May you always feel His presence and His hand and may you and yours be safe from all end-time evil.

ACKNOWLEDGMENTS

A special appreciation to all my ministry team and partners for their prayers and support. To Mary and Adam Cuevas, for their part in launching this book. Donna Ferguson for her editing skills, Kimberly Stewart of Pneuma Life Publishing and Christian Living Books for her dedication to excellence and Albert C. Sandoval III for the "Prophetic Power of the Hour" cover design. May the Lord fill your lives with His essence.

"The Prophetic Power of the Hour"

It is the night of the morning

"Prepare for Daybreak"

ENDORSEMENTS

"Much before I was aware of God's revelation to Irma, The Lord had instructed us to begin a prayer meeting from 5:00 a.m. to 7:00 a.m. every morning in our ministry centre in Tel Aviv, Israel. That prayer meeting is making many things happen. There is MUCH power released as we harmonize in prayer at the time of the Fourth Watch. Irma's book contains VITAL revelation for the release of the Glory of God to cover the earth as the waters cover the sea."

–Pastor Dominiquae Bierman
Kehilat Har Tsion
Network of Messianic Congregations
Kad-Esh MAP Ministries
Israel

"The Prophetic Power of the Hour" is like a banquet table prepared for us in the presence of our enemies, and Reverend Irma Diaz provides us with some of the most spiritually nourishing food I've ever tasted. Those of us who want to accomplish something of eternal value for God during these troubled, but opportune times, have much to gain from the revelation contained in this book."

–Donna Ferguson
Author and President of "No Neutral Ground Ministries"
Newport Beach, California

"Rev. Irma Diaz is a fresh and timely voice in these days of spiritual confusion. She brings the body of Christ clear and sound Biblical truth for today. The need for fresh manna is just as necessary now as it was for the children of Israel in their wilderness. I recommend that you read this present work as manna from Heaven for our time. This work will help untie the knots of spiritual misnomers that are common in the Christian marketplace. Irma Diaz trumpets a powerful insight into some cloudy and unsure waters in the Church today. Read this book with an expectation of revelation knowledge that will fill you with powerful spiritual enrichment!"

–Dr. Ed Kuhn
President of the Rock Ministry Training Center
Gainesville, Georgia

"The depth of Irma Diaz's insights and knowledge of Biblical truth presents a dynamic illumination to the Word of God from which everyone can be inspired and even convicted. Her depth of study and spiritual discernment brings forth a strong anointing of God's wisdom and Word as we approach the close of this age and the return of the crucified Christ."

–Tony Nassif
Author of *Jesus, Politics and the Church*
Los Angeles, California

"God is releasing His prophetic voice to the Body of Christ at this critical time in Church History. Irma Diaz is one of those voices. She combines sound Biblical truth with her prophetic gifting to bring fresh revelation necessary for the Church to accomplish its eternal purposes at the close of this age. This book will inspire you to a new level of faith and commitment to pursue our Lord with all your heart."

–Lonny Robbins
Senior Pastor
Trinity Fellowship Church
Mayor
Pampa, Texas.

CONTENTS

INTRODUCTION

The Bible contains so much instruction for the victorious Christian life, yet many in the Church today continue to live in defeat. There is also a frustration in many believers because they never seem to finish what they start.

If you are anything like me, you want to know what effect your life is having for God, and in the lives of others. It has always been difficult for me to be consistent with the things of God unless I know I'm being effective. It's not enough for someone to tell me I'm effective; I need to know that I am, and the only way I can know this is if I understand what I'm doing.

As I wrote this book, I was quite inspired. I was determined that once completed, this book would accomplish its God-ordained task-to effect this generation, and many generations to come. That helped me remain consistent in my effort. No matter where I ministered throughout the world, I took every opportunity to pick up my laptop to fulfill God's will for this book, expecting to see the finished product. I was able to stay focused, believing that at the end I'd see the vision fulfilled.

Having *knowledge* is different than having *understanding*. You obtain knowledge in your head, but you understand with your heart. Formal education is a wonderful beginning, but until you grasp the concept and meaning with your heart, all it will ever be is knowledge.

When we acquire knowledge through secular education, it is difficult to break the mold of man-made parameters. There are those who hear a message, but have no ability for expansion because they filter what they hear through these man-made parameters. They have knowledge but no understanding. Knowledge is usually visible while understanding is invisible.

I know that the Spirit of the Lord is omnipresent because I've been taught from the Word of God and reliable Biblical commentaries that He is. However, to understand that the Spirit of the Lord is everywhere, well now, this is an invisible situation that must take me into the realm of revelation.

If I can grasp that, then, and only then, will this knowledge become effective. It is my desire, through this writing, to impart a supernatural understanding to others through what the Lord has shown me. In order to do this effectively I must go back to the basics from the heart of God.

This mission has possessed my destiny, and has imparted to my heart an understanding, which enables me and causes me to be effective. For years, the Body of Christ has preached about the importance of fasting, prayer, music and worship. We are filled with knowledge, but in many cases little understanding.

It is no longer enough for me to tithe because someone told me that I'd be cursed if I didn't. It is no longer enough to worship Him because I have been told He is worthy, or to serve in the church because it builds character. The Spirit of the Lord is saying, "There is more." Can't you feel there is more?

We love not because we feel it, but because He tells us to. Obedience is far better than sacrifice (Deuteronomy 26:16; I Samuel 15:22). We obey because He is God and that is not negotiable. He is God and His dimensions are never-ending.

> The secret things belong unto the LORD our God: but those things which are revealed belong unto us and to our children for ever, that we may do all the words of this law.
>
> (Deuteronomy 29:29)

I am aware of Deuteronomy 29:29 and realize that there are some things that will be beyond our understanding until we reach glory. However, don't you want to go as deep into His heart as you can?

There has been a great deal of talk about entering a new dispensation of time–a new window of opportunity in which God wants to accomplish new things through your hand. However, its not enough to just be alive at this new time and place; you must live within it effectively, for HIM and only HIM. My desire for this book is to infuse you with a hunger that will take you to great heights in spite of yourself. Your limitations are in your imagination.

> When I was a child, I spoke as a child, I understood as a child, I thought as a child; but when I became a man, I put away childish things. For now, we see in a glass, darkly; but then, face to face: now I know in part; but then shall I know even as also I am known. (I Corinthians 13:11,12)

It is obvious that there is a constant progression from "glory to glory." It's not enough for you to read or hear prophecy; you must desire the ability to understand the invisible/spiritual in its proper dimension and time. I'm not speaking of understanding as the world knows it, but of the deep inner understanding that brings the revelation into sight. You don't have to understand all the theological things of God to be blessed by them. In other words, you can attain it.

We must ask God to give us the highest possible achievement in this area. We know from the different spiritual positions in the body of Christ that there are different measures of understanding.

And he gave some, apostles; and some, prophets; and some, evangelists; and some, pastors and teachers; For the perfecting of the saints, for the work of the ministry, for the edifying of the body of Christ. (Ephesians 4:11,12)

Nevertheless, we must go as deep as we can, regardless of the measure allotted to us. I write spirit to spirit; receive in like manner, beloved.

You cannot grasp God with your limited, finite mind. None of us can. Ask Him to breath upon you His Breath that you might be enabled by His fullness; and don't be concerned about what level or measure you'll be given. For He is a God Who will fill your heart with a knowing (*yada*)–we'll get into that later–that will lead you to the fulfillment of your destiny.

The devil doesn't want you to succeed. He'll do everything he can to deter you from your destiny. From the Jewish perspective, when you are not walking in purpose–when your timing is always off–it is as though you are deleting words from the promises of God in the Holy Scriptures. This means that although you know the Lord, you are living a defeated life. When you walk in purpose, and in God's will, you become one of the most influential people possible.

As you journey through the pages of this book your eyes will be opened to many key things, four of these are as follows:

- The time we are now in
- God's order of things
- The power of influence
- Attachment to God

When I speak of the time we are in, please note that I understand that there is one, our own personal time in the fulfillment of destiny, and two, the constant corporate time for the Church. I believe both are important. You have a purpose, a destiny, and a timing for fulfillment. Your promises travel through space to meet you at a certain place in your life, and if you are in His will, you will be there to meet them.

It is not by observation that you discern when the fulfillment is coming, for the Kingdom of God cannot be discerned by observation. Jesus, Himself said, "An evil adulterous generation seeketh after a sign. (Matthew 12: 39a) In verse 37, Jesus says, *"For by thy words thou shalt be justified, and by thy words thou shalt be condemned."*

Jesus is about to prophesy His resurrection as the sign to them. The Spirit of Prophecy releases fulfillment, not the signs in the sky. We may not know every unfolding moment, but we will always have the *"Power of the Hour"* revealed to us. It will unfold by the revelatory Spirit of Prophecy, which I believe is available for every believer.

> And I fell at his feet to worship him. And he said unto me, See thou do it not: I am thy fellow servant, and of thy brethren that have the testimony of Jesus: worship God: for the testimony of Jesus is the spirit of prophecy. (Revelation 19:10)

Chapter One

THE NIGHT WATCHES

Discerning the Time

Depending on your sphere of influence within the Church, you may have already heard of the Third Day Dispensation. I preached my first message on the Third Day at Pastor Glen Berteau's Church, Calvary Temple Worship Center, in Modesto, California in 1996.

This concept is based on the fact that one day is as a thousand years to the Lord (II Peter 3:8). I didn't understand it fully myself at the time, but I knew that the Lord was saying to me, "This is the inauguration of the Third Day."

Then, the Lord began to speak to me about a change in time. This change would affect the course of nature and be based on His people, believers in Christ. What intrigued me the most was that He made it clear to me that it would be caused by His people all over the world. This change of time is as a shifting from one intention to another, from one mindset to another, and from one reality to another.

Two thousand years have come and gone since our Lord Jesus Christ died for all creation. This puts us on the threshold of the Third Day. Certainly, the Lord has His time clock, but we know that for some reason, things are subject to change.

I don't know about you, but this creates a curiosity in me that I must satisfy with the measure of answers given to me from His Spirit. I believe this curiosity is strategically placed inside us to draw us closer and closer to Him as we search. There is no doubt in my mind that we are in a dispensational shift into a fullness of times, and that He is stirring the Church with the "missing links" of today through deeper revelation.

> That in the dispensation of the fulness of times he might gather together in one all things in Christ, both which are in heaven, and which are on earth; even in him. (Ephesians 1:10)

The Division of Day and Night

The Church is called to accomplish certain things within a block of time, and as we consider *The Prophetic Power of the Hour*, there is something else that is key to our understanding. A day and night are divided into parts according to Genesis 1. Very simply, the Lord created night and day. For example, the day is divided into two parts: morning and afternoon; and nighttime into two parts: evening and midnight, which begins the illumination of the new day.

I continue to stir with curiosity as to why the Lord created time in this fashion. As I study the Scriptures, I find many passages regarding the division of the day and the night, including specific times allotted for prayer. The Holy Scriptures tell us this:

> Thou makest darkness and it is night: wherein all the beasts of the forest do creep, the young lions roar after their prey and seek their meat from God. The sun ariseth, they gather themselves together and lay them down in their dens. Man goeth forth into his work and to his labor until the evening. (Psalms 104:20-23)

> And it came to pass in those days, that He went out into the mountain to pray and continued all night in prayer to God. (Luke 6:12)

> Ye are all the Children of light, and the children of the day, we are not of the night, not of darkness. (I Thessalonians 5:5)

Might I submit to you that according to Scripture, the focus and power of the day in which we live is on the division of it. And, the attention we give to the order of it will cause the deepest revelation of it. In understanding the prophetic, we need to dissect the message of the hour for as much depth as is humanly possible.

In biblical history, the watches of the night were crucial. For example, the Jews had three watches: evening, midnight to 3:00 a.m., and morning. Morning was considered the third watch, which was later changed by the Romans to four watches. Let us pay special attention to these verses in Mark 13:

> But of that day and that hour knoweth no man, no, not the angels which are in heaven, neither the son, but the father. Take heed, watch and pray: for ye know not when the time is. For the son of man is as a man taking a far journey who left his house, and gave authority to his servants and to every man his work and commanded the porter to watch. Watch ye therefore; for ye know not when the master of the house cometh, at even, or in the midnight, or at the cockcrowing, or in the morning: Lest coming suddenly he find you sleeping. And what I say unto you, I say to all, Watch. (Mark 13:32-37)

The Four Watches

Notice, first of all, that no one knows-not even the angels-when He is coming. Also, notice the four watches our Lord mentions:

- Sunset to midnight
- Midnight, the awakening of the new day
- Cockcrowing/between midnight and 3:00 a.m.
- Morning, which is 3:00 a.m. to 6:00 a.m./daybreak

Duty called at these intervals of the night–but why? We can't deny that everything within the Bible is written for a specific reason. Whether based on a first dimensional interpretation, i.e. time, place and considerations, and/or something deeper, it's there for a reason. The Word is alive! It existed in the beginning of time and always will, because it supernaturally fits into all things ordained by God. It is the necessary ingredient into which every moment of time must fit.

> For the word of God is quick, and powerful, and sharper than any two edged sword, piercing even to the dividing asunder of soul and spirit, and of the joints and marrow, and is a discerner of the thoughts and intents of the heart. (Hebrews 4:12).

The Word tells us that we all stand naked and opened in front of Him (Hebrews 4:13). Because of what the Lord has shown me regarding the Third Day, I believe we are in the process of a change; however, midnight is the awakening of a new day, not daybreak. This is why people all over the world, including the Jews, tend to celebrate a New Year at midnight. If you will recall, Jesus prayed for long periods during this block of time. It was at the third and fourth watch that His concentrated prayer was sent to the Father.

The Interpretation of Prophetic Time

When you interpret Scripture, there is prophetic language as well as a dimension that goes beyond the literal. Today could mean one thousand years to us. The many metaphors/parables presented to us indicate that things have much deeper meanings. I am convinced that God desires that we dig as deep as we can.

To bring balance to that last sentence, please understand that as a Bible student, you should dig with supervision so as not to go beyond what is intended. I've seen people get lost in stretched interpretations, which can eventually be very dangerous. We must stick with what is solid, yet not be afraid to let God show us the deeper, timely truths of His living Word.

> Jesus prayed most of the time "while it was still dark." And in the morning, rising up a great while before day, He went out, and departed into a solitary place, and there prayed. (Mark 1:35)

This time slot was prior to daybreak, and more than likely after midnight-as after midnight is considered morning. If we are going to interpret the prophetic time as a day (a thousand years), let us understand that it begins at midnight. There is power in understanding this because it helps us discern what we are supposed to be doing.

I believe that we are now living in the third/fourth watch of the night–the morning that will birth daybreak. Although you may think this is a stretch. If you look for it, you will find that every day and night recorded in the Bible was accompanied by some indication of the time it was in, at that particular moment.

For example, at this very moment, while I'm writing, it's Friday night, almost midnight. I'm typing with an awareness that Friday is almost over and it will soon be a new day. Now I begin to think about sleeping, not because I'm sleepy, but because it's necessary that I consider what I have to do tomorrow.

I'm moving beyond the awareness of Friday and looking ahead to the next day. This causes me to be effective in the present in such a way as to benefit the future. Likewise, we must know the time within the day in which we are living so we can be effective, in the present time, for the future.

> The first day of the week cometh Mary Magdalene early, when it was yet dark, unto the sepulchre, and seeth the stone taken away from the sepulchre. (John 20:1)

At this very moment in time, we are getting ready to see the light of the new day. In John 20:1 (in the Third Day), Mary Magdalene came to the sepulcher while it was still dark (morning) and saw the stone rolled away.

In Matthew 14:25, it was in the fourth watch (before daybreak) that Jesus came to them (His disciples) walking on water. The fourth watch is the morning that still finds itself in darkness, but slowly begins to show the light of the new day. In Matthew 26:34, Scripture records that Jesus told Peter he would deny him three times before the cock crowed that night. The whole testing and trial of Jesus and His disciples took place at night. If anything, this should create a curiosity in us to understand why. We also see this in Hosea:

> Come and let us return unto the Lord; for He hath torn and He will heal us; He hath smitten, and He will bind us up, after two days will He revive us: in the third day He will raise us up, and we shall live in His sight. Then shall we know, if we follow on to know the Lord: His going forth is prepared as the morning; and He shall come unto us as the rain, as the latter and the former rain unto the earth. (Hosea 6:1-3)

Notice the declaration that He smites but He revives and restores that which He tears down. Nothing happens without His approval. This speaks of the rebuilding of the Third Temple. He will save us from the two sanctuaries. Those with spiritual ears and eyes, make note of the depth of that thought.

Ephraim and Judah

We as a Church, have gone through a great deal in the last two days in our sanctuaries, but on the Third Day, the third time, He will revive and restore us. Curiously, in verse 3, He begins to speak through the prophet of His going forth as the morning. We will truly come to know Him on this special day. Just as we know that the dawning of a new day comes whether we expect it or not, He will come like rain; and, as the rain satisfies the earth, there will be a satisfaction throughout the earth.

In verse 4, He speaks of Ephraim and Judah-as He did in Ezekiel 37:15. You may remember that Ephraim, one of Joseph's sons, received the double portion blessing from his grandfather, Jacob, who adopted he and his brother, Manasseh, as sons (Genesis 48:5).

Judah, though the fourth son of Jacob, ended up receiving his father's blessing and scepter as leader of all the tribes (Genesis 49:3-10). There was a never-ending contention and great envy between the two in the time of Judges; but in Ezekiel, the prophet is told that they will be reunited in brotherly love (Ezekiel 5:32).

> Ephraim what shall I do unto thee? O Judah, what shall I do unto thee? For your goodness is as a morning cloud, and as the early dew it goeth away. Therefore have I hewed them by the prophets; I have slain them by the words of my mouth: and thy judgments are as the light that goeth forth.
>
> (Hosea 6:4,5)

His love for Ephraim and Judah causes Him to wonder how He will pass a judgment upon them. These are brothers in division. In verse 5, He refers to the prophets, and speaks of hewn words, meaning that the Lord gave the prophets a word to speak and they did not, they held back. God have mercy on all of us.

> But they like men have transgressed the covenant: there have they dealt treacherously against me. (Hosea 6:7)

According to Scripture, there was spiritual adultery, a great transgression of the covenant. Now as this Third Day approaches, God has a dilemma. "It is hard for Me," says the Lord, "for I must cast a verdict on My people. Both Ephraim and Jacob transgressed. What shall I do with them? I will revive after two days and I will raise them up in the Third Day."

The Third Day was awakened by midnight and we have all felt it. The Church is now standing in the duty of the third/fourth watch, which is the very presence of the Third Day. We can only see by revelation the light breaking forth, but it is still dark. We must watch and pray!

The Light of Daybreak

How long will we speak of the Church (Ephraim and Jacob) coming together as one—or of the tearing down of the racial walls of diversity rallies, which are prophesying what is to be? I believe there are people in leadership positions within denominations and church organizations (fellowships), who have seen prophetically (by revelation) the light of daybreak.

The light of daybreak begins to shed light on the matter. In some cases, these are the people who see the wrong-doings and injustices; they see the politics and the marketing of the people of God; they know what is wrong and do not speak up, just because they are afraid to be ousted. They are as those prophets who had the Word of the Lord hewn in them and they held it and did not release it. Let the fear of the Lord be upon us! Let the mercy of God be poured out on all of us as Leaders in this crucial hour.

We cannot fit into a mold, and we cannot be what others want us to be. And, for those playing God, I must advise you, you cannot oust a spiritual office; you cannot oust the anointing; and no one can take away the spiritual gifts. A Board of Directors cannot strip you of who God made you to be. I am who I am. You are who you are. God is looking for those who will speak up and be a part of leading God's people into "daybreak".

I'm tired of hearing about unity, as I know you are. I want to experience it. We cannot enter into certain moments in time without it. The Power in the Hour is recognizing it! The third/fourth watch calls for just that, "watch".

Yes, there are victories, and God does show Himself; however, it is a time for preparation. The day has been awakened by midnight and we feel the "daybreak" near. We are in the night of the morning. There is a process in time so important that it had to be documented in creation, and it continues to be mentioned throughout the Holy Scriptures.

The Morning Dew

> My children, your goodness is as a morning cloud and just like the early dew of the fourth watch, it goes away. (Hosea 6:4).

Dew is a symbol of life and abundance. The people of Israel depended on the dew during the long hot summers. Regions were blessed to have dew mornings, just as cities will be blessed when there is unity among the people of God.

The Lord spoke this message to me which is based in Hosea 6:4: *"I have given you the dew of the morning for daybreak and it is as goodness to rain on you and it will never burn away. What shall I do unto you, O Ephraim and Judah, what will I do with you? For we are entering a time when I will raise you up, for it is then that you shall know Me and My going forth like the morning. If you heed the time within the time, I will cause the dew to become rain, latter and former and it will not cease, for I desire mercy (that you know Me) and not sacrifice. You must know of Me more than of burnt offerings yea, this is the time of recompense, prepare for daybreak."*

Make no mistake beloved, just because the Church has heard the message preached on unity does not mean we have grasped it. It is the fourth watch of the night and daybreak is almost here.

Watch and Pray

We must look within before we can see without. What did Jesus mean when He said, *"watch and pray?"* We've been indoctrinated to believe that this speaks of our surroundings. Although this may have something to do with it, this is only the first dimension of interpretation. Many are so busy looking at their surroundings that they are missing the watch of the morning while it is yet dark. To watch is to look within before you can see without (see Matthew 26:41, Mark 13:32-37).

The Power of the Prophetic Hour is understanding the watch of the night we are in prior to fulfillment. In other words, all the cycles in our lives have a night and day. I, for example, have promises within my heart. Personally, one promise might be ready for daybreak, while another might be barely approaching midnight. If I can understand that, I will be much more effective.

Corporately in this hour, however, I believe the Lord has us preparing for the light of day. He is wanting repentance from you and me at this very moment. He is wanting a look within.

There are so many unresolved issues within the Church, and if we don't begin to pull on the womb of God's heart, we will not experience what we could in our lifetime as the Church. I believe that, corporately, it is time to look within to prepare for daybreak. We are so captivated with what has been prophesied by modern-day prophets that we miss out on the dawning of fulfillment. To every prophetic utterance there is a dawning time and if we miss that, we miss the power of it as it breaks forth.

The Influence of Time

If you remember nothing else, remember this: *Prophecy is not ful-filled by a human date*, but in the *"influence of time."* It is a release of influence to establish on earth what has been recorded in Heaven.

We don't know the exact time in which we live, but we do know the season. We can't go by a human calendar; we must go by the spiritual calendar of influence. There must first be a "dawning" time, and the moments before this are crucial, for this is your direction and your under-standing of time.

O My Lord, what a time we are in–an opportune time. Daybreak is almost here; however, unless the Church steps into the time there will be no manifestation of the Third Day. Any new dispensation brings with it the fulfillment of prophecy, and prophecy is only ours for the unveiling of Christ to the world (Revelation 19:10). Only when His Body, Ephraim and Judah, come together, will the unveiling of Christ occur. It is the Creator longing for the attachment of His creation.

Chapter Two

THE REVIVING OF THE 3rd TEMPLE

Preparing for Daybreak

The following is not intended as a teaching on the historical life of the temple–that would deviate from our focus. My intention is to deposit in you the prophetic concept I believe is helpful. The first temple was built by Solomon (I Kings 8 and II Chronicles 5), and destroyed during the days of Nebuchadnezzar (II Kings 25:8).

Those returning from exile, during the time of Zerubbabel attempted to build a replica of the temple, but were too poor to do it justice (Ezra 3:12). All along, their eyes had been on the beauty of the structure. The day came in the 18th year of King Herod that he decided to complete the rebuilding of what was known as the Third Temple, but the focus remained on the structure and its man-made efforts.

Later, Jesus prophesied the destruction of this building (see Matthew 24:2). This was a prophetic hour of fulfillment. First, there was a speaking forth of the plan, the writing of the plan, then the action, and finally the fulfillment.

In John 2:19 Jesus said, *"Destroy this temple and in three days, I will raise it up."* In verse 21, He confirms that He was speaking of His body.

> He is the head of the Body, the Church: who is the beginning, the firstborn from the dead; that in all things He might have the preeminence. (Colossians 1:18)

The Prophetic Dimensions

Let us take the prophetic dimensions. First and foremost, the Lord knew very well that they understood the importance of the temple–Herod had taken 46 years to build it. How in the world could this man think He could raise it up again in three days?

The first dimension of interpretation is the one taught in Bible school, which is time, place, and considerations. Of course, He knew how to make them understand, even when they attempted to ignore the witness they felt inside. Their focus throughout past generations had been the material richness of the temple; hence missing the whole point.

In John 2:26, He told them they had turned His Father's house into a house of merchandise. Obviously the focus of the leaders was on prosperity–making money in the house of the Lord–and they were teaching all the people to do the same. The leaders were merchandising and our Lord was disgusted and angered.

We believe that God wants us to prosper, but this does not mean our focus should be on prosperity. This is why many of you have had a sour taste in your mouth. If you focus on prosperity, you will eventually merchandise your ministries and/or the temple of the Lord. You do not tithe to get rich; you tithe because you love God. If you get rich because of it, praise His Holy Name, but that is not your focus.

The principle of monetary sowing and reaping will work because it is biblical. However, our focus is to be on what is expected when one stands on any promise in the Word of God. We are to give with faith. Let me agree and clarify this by saying that to focus on something means that it holds your attention. To expect something means that you anticipate or believe in it. What an insult to the Holiness of God to allow our attention to be placed on our return, instead of on our love for Him. I will leave this "thought expressed" in God's hands.

The second dimension of interpretation is the one taught in our salvation message: Jesus died, was buried, and on the Third Day He rose again, defeating death, hell and the grave. This is the foundation of our belief unto eternal life. He was the temple He spoke of, and they did indeed destroy it, and on the Third Day it rose from destruction. This was no longer a material matter, but a spiritual matter; because once He ascended on high, there was a transformation of His body, which leads us to the third dimension of that "truth."

> Know ye not that ye are the temple of God and that the
> Spirit of God dwelleth in you? (I Corinthians 3:16)

When He left, we became His body here on earth, hence becoming His temple. When we speak of rebuilding the Third Temple, we are really referring to reviving. Because, on the Third Day, when He rose from the dead, the Third Day temple foundation was set.

> After two days He will revive us: in the Third Day He will
> raise us up, and we shall live in His sight. (Hosea 6:2)

This is an amazing phenomenon. We become His body and His temple as He dwells within us. When, then, is the Third Temple, the body of Christ, revived? It is on the Third Day.

It is after the two days that the temple is revived (is awakened). In the Third Day He will raise us up (rebuild and restore us). This brings me to the prophetic message of the third/fourth watch; right now, the focus must be within.

When we construct a building, we do it from the outside in. When God builds, He does it from the inside out. During this Night Watch, God is reviving and rebuilding upon the foundation that was torn down, as prophesied in Hosea 6:1-3. It is not so much what is around us during this watch, but what is within us.

There must be a preparation for daybreak. He is reviving the Third Temple (His Church) from the inside out upon the foundation He left for it. He began in the Genesis of time with a heart-throb for souls. As a lover speaks to His beloved and says, "Come forth, my love", He spoke into you and said, "Come forth, my love." And, in a moment, you came forth, with an amazing capacity to love when you may never have been taught how.

The Bible says we are fearfully and wonderfully made. Yes, each of us is an incredible piece of holy art. I am a phenomenon. You are a phenomenon. And that which He created shall be revived and raised up. The Spirit of the Lord will again say, "Come forth my love" and we will be resurrected as a phenomenon, into the Third Day. This is not knowledge, but an understanding of that which is not yet manifested to the natural eye. This is the invisible, manifested as revelation.

The Father's Business

In Luke 2:41, we find Jesus as a twelve-year-old boy, attending the feast of the Passover with His parents. Can you imagine the feelings He must have had as a young man? He had learned about the Passover lamb and watched as it was slain, knowing deep in His heart that this action would bring about the fulfillment of prophecy. He was the Passover Lamb for the world, and for this purpose He had entered the womb of creation.

When the feast of the Passover ended and families prepared to return to their homes, Jesus became separated from His parents. And it came to pass that after three days they found Him in the temple, leaving everyone in awe of His understanding of the Scriptures. His parents said to Him, "Why did you do this to us?" He replied, "How is it that ye sought me? Wist ye not that I must be about my Father's business?" (vs. 49) And the Bible says they did not understand Him. His response was very simple: it was His Father's house, and His Father's business, and He was tending to it.

The Kingdom of God is Within

Today is the third/fourth watch of the Third Day, and many are looking for Jesus without when He is within. He is reviving the Third Temple. The Lord says that after Three Days, those looking around them will find Him in the temple. This is the Father's business. The Church is too busy, and this busyness has led us outward instead of inward. This doesn't mean we are not to work and build the Kingdom, but the Kingdom of God is within us.

The issue is souls, creation, and the attachment of creation to their Creator. Look in the temple and you will find Him. Look within and you will hear His voice as never before. Look within and you will be amazed at the interior of the phenomenon of creation. You will find Him about His Father's business, rebuilding souls that have been torn down. After Three Days, we shall be revived, and when we are, we will look back and cringe at our past focus. Take heed to "truth".

The Dominating Culture Within the Temple

As I watch, I find a dominating culture that breeds ugliness within the temple. I'm referring to the culture of dress, jargon, clicks and learned behavior. These are the "interior designers" within the temple: they dress the best, sound the best, and hang out with the right people. For the record, there is nothing wrong with dressing well; but for some, if you can't dress a certain way, you will never fit in.

As you look a little closer, their smiles are so beautiful, their behavior so very proper. They fit in so well with what we've been told we are supposed to look like, that now we begin to notice people trying to dress like them, act like them, and sound like them in order to become a part of the elitist click. You hear people calling it impartation!

A closer look reveals something about the décor that you never noticed before-rejection. You see hurting people feeling more and more inadequate because they are not accepted by the dominating culture. The "accepted" seem to do everything better; they even sound better when they pray or speak.

You think this is all right because they are so anointed, so sure of themselves, and they reek of authority. Then, you realize that something is not right. You look to the leaders and see that they are the designers of the interior decor. You either make a decision to keep trying to fit in, no matter what; or, you stop staring at them in awe and begin to call sin, sin and hurt, hurt.

Décor Favors the Designer

You may become so nauseated with the hypocrisy that you leave, thinking you'll find a different scenario elsewhere, only to find the same dominating culture throughout the Church. So you stay and begin to sow seeds of discord against them, which now brings you into the dominating culture. Congratulations! You are now a bonafide member of the disgusting in God's eyes.

The interior designers no longer view you as a team player, so you might as well forget about becoming a part of anything significant unless you surpass them. This releases the spirit of competition within the disgusting, elitist clicks. Unfortunately, this is just one example of this décor.

For just as you have different rooms in a house, there are different rooms with different décors. And, just as there are houses in different areas-upper, middle to upper, middle, lower class- the décor favors the designer. For example, an impoverished Church will not accept prosperity; a legalistic Church sees everything that doesn't fall into their criteria as dirty/sinful.

Of course, anyone is free to leave and go where they fit in, but this is not the way God intended the temple to be. Please do not be offended with my blatant honesty, but the Lord showed me that within the temple, during this time of rebuilding and preparing for day break, there would be an opportunity for this dominating culture to repent and humble themselves before God. He said He would bring in voices that He could trust to bring in truth. Our Lord is not pleased with our mother's milk as a Church, and desires that we be fully nourished by the meat of His Truth.

We have conveyed the wrong concept in the temple. You can't be full of yourself and have room for God. The time for "house cleaning" is here. He is raising up individuals that do not operate as cowards. I'm not referring to disrespecting leaders or creating chaos because you are not getting your way. I'm referring to true prophets who will not pull punches. They are about their Father's business, preparing for daybreak, rebuilding from the inside out.

With some of the things we've seen, can you blame a sinner for not wanting to stay in the Church? The antidote for this is not to run from the dominating culture, but to pierce it with the light that exposes the sin, idolatry and the hidden agendas of mankind.

The Root of Creation

As I studied creation, I found some very profound truths. All of creation has a root. This phenomenon begins on the inside; and before we can know the outside, we must know the inside of creation.

In the Jewish perspective of interpretation and teaching, it is said that all of humanity has an evil inclination as well as a good inclination. This means that every one of us has a tendency toward evil as well as good. And even those in the Church, who consider themselves pious and holy, have tendencies toward evil that they must combat daily.

I've noticed this truth in myself whenever I'm tempted to join in on a conversation about somebody. There are even those who, deep in their hearts, tend to want to hear the worst about an individual. This is when the self appointed policemen in the Church rise up—those who are always looking for something that will taint the image of others. This is an evil inclination from the root. The only way we overcome it is to overcome evil with good.

There are people in the Church who love God and truly want to serve Him, yet are in bondage to this evil inclination. I speak of clergy as well as laity. Because these individuals are viewed with respect, few notice it; and those who do will very seldom confront it.

This is why many are in turmoil over their secret condition. When you feel anger, unforgiveness, lust, jealousy or envy, it doesn't mean you are evil, it means that your evil inclination is attempting to overtake you, and it will, if you let it. It only becomes evil when you act on your evil inclination.

We have all experienced this in our walk with God. It's nothing to be ashamed of unless you allow it to overtake you. Evil must be overcome by good and the only way this can happen is if one looks "within" first. The more we overcome this evil inclination, the more good becomes a part of our thoughts and ways.

You can have eternal life and still be in bondage to your evil inclination. You may grow in the knowledge of His Word, but never understand why you are not happy as a Christian believer. In our "watchfulness" we must deal with our evil inclination before we can truly reap the benefits of "daybreak" on the Third Day.

Providence

There are three parts/elements within the root of our creation. The first of these is PROVIDENCE. The Lord has spoken His purpose into all of creation's root. When I pondered on this He began to speak to me about the prophetic promises dwelling in my root that have not yet been fulfilled.

> Behold, the former things are come to pass, and new things do I declare: before they spring forth I tell you of them. (Isaiah 42:9)

He told me to go out and tell those who would listen that the promises of providence are within them. Your destiny and purpose have already been created within your root. This was done prophetically by God, before you were created. You just haven't seen it all come to pass.

> So shall my word be that goeth forth out of my mouth: it shall not return unto me void, but it shall accomplish that which I please, and it shall prosper in the thing whereto I sent it. (Isaiah 55:11).

The prophetic ministers and those who are called to speak into your life are merely confirming what is already in your root. We see how these promises grew when the Messiah was promised to Mother Israel.

The prophets prophesied throughout history until the fullness of times came for the promise. The spoken prophetic word sets things in motion and causes them to spring forth. There are those appointed in your life to pull the substance of the root out of you. We may not see the manifestation of what is spoken immediately because of the issue of providence and God's order and system, but it has been set in motion and it will accomplish what it is supposed to accomplish.

The Image of God

The second element within our root is the IMAGE OF GOD. According to Genesis 2:7, He formed man from the dust of the ground, breathed into his nostrils the breath of life, and man became a living soul. The impartation of the image of God is "within", not without. His image is His glory–the glory of His creation. Within your root is the image and glory of God. What a baffling thought.

Through the years, we have developed our own image. People look at us a certain way, but God is going to restore His image here on earth and His glory will rise upon us.

> Arise, shine; for thy light is come, and the glory of the LORD is risen upon thee. For, behold, the darkness shall cover the earth, and gross darkness the people: but the LORD shall arise upon thee, and his glory shall be seen upon thee. (Isaiah 60:1,2).

I reiterate, the glory of God is within, not without. In this hour, God wants to show Himself to the world–and the way He has selected to do this is through His Body, the Third Temple.

The Revelation of God

The third element within our root is the REVELATION OF GOD. This is the revelation that takes us from glory to glory. We are the only species on earth that can make a choice. If we get on the right road and draw closer to God, revelation becomes a part of our life. If we don't, we will never experience the revelation that makes a deep impression upon one's life. Once we come to know our Messiah, Jesus Christ, we cannot help but want to draw closer to Him. Walking away will cause great darkness.

If you are wondering why God would place good and evil into His creation, you must first understand why you were created. You were created to draw close to Him. You were created for love's sake–for a relationship with Him. It is His grace that causes you misery when you walk away. He desired you to make a choice.

The choice is not just salvation, although this is the most important, but the choice must go deeper. You must want to see the purposes of God fulfilled. You must want to have the image of your Father shine through you, and the glory of God to be upon you. You must want it so badly that you will check what is within and make some choices.

His desire is to pull out of you what was intended from the beginning. This is the preparation for daybreak of the Third Day–a focus within. Don't look to your ministry or your Pastor to do it for you; don't look to your spouse.

This is the hour to "work out your own salvation (and your changes) with fear and trembling." (Philippians 2:12). There is a preparation going on. Deal with your evil inclination, believe God for your destiny, draw close to Him and see the glory of God arise upon you!

Jesus said, *"Destroy this temple and in three days I will raise it up again."* Did they think for one moment that the image and glory of His creation would remain hidden? Did they think they could stop the promises of God? Now is the time. The reviving of the Third Temple is within; and within this Third Day temple is a root that inhabits the promises of our Creator.

In you is the image of God, the glory that God desires to manifest and revive. But, in you is an evil and a good inclination. To deal with it you must ask yourself what is evil to you? What I'm finding is that many things that are evil to our Lord are not evil to the local Church. As we prepare, we must ask ourselves what we call evil. Herod used the ministers of that day to build/revive, and today God is using His ministers to build/revive. They are going about their Father's business.

I write to you about the mysteries of the last days. He who has an ear, let Him hear what the Spirit of the Lord is saying through His builders. The Prophetic Power of the Hour is not knowing what was said because you heard it, but knowing what you heard because you understand it in your heart.

There is a dimensional interpretation that is key to what the prophets of today are saying. The prophecy becomes powerful in your life personally when you apply the depth of it to your life. It is today, but today has details to it that could make all the difference in your present and in your future. Within you is a root of great treasure. You have the ability within you to effect that which is without.

Prepare for Daybreak

The Third Day will have an effect upon the world without. Judgment begins in the house of the Lord, and in order for us to see, the light of truth must pierce the temple within. If we stop and think about the people in the Church, those who are in schism, those who have been hurt by Church members, can we honestly say that we, as a Church, have been operating from our good inclination? Good must over take evil.

How many backsliders are back on the street because of something we did or said? Granted, there are many with such deep issues that they become overly sensitive and in their ignorance leave the Lord because of someone else. However, if we could overcome our evil inclination we would be more tolerant and more prayerful.

If, as a leader, you cannot gracefully be confronted with an insult to your ego without reciprocating the ignorance, you are allowing your evil inclination to get the best of you. You don't have to defend yourself. God is your defender! As laity in the Church, if you've been hurt by a leader and are trying to prove them wrong or make them look bad, you've been overtaken by the evil inclination in your root.

Don't you see that by not defending yourself, by not having to prove your point, everything within your root begins to spring forth like the morning? Jesus could have destroyed them all. He could have called a legion of angels to destroy the entire city but He stayed His hand. Prepare for daybreak!

Chapter Three

THE POWER OF INFLUENCE
A Holy Partnership

A few years back, as the prophetic gift came out of seclusion and was welcomed back to the pulpits, I believe that even the most well intended ministers began to attempt to narrow down dates and times. Please do not misunderstand, when speaking of prophecy I do believe that God can speak to you about a day, but in most cases, one day is as a thousand years. The word usually represents the seasons.

In chapter one, I mentioned that prophecy is not fulfilled by a human date, but in the influence of time. The prophetic Third Day everyone speaks of does not happen because it is the first of January. I want to be careful to say that the Lord can do whatever He wants to.

He may tell someone something will change on a certain human day, but there is for example a Gregorian calendar and a Hebrew calendar to consider. To a Jew for example, the New Year falls on Rosh Hashanah, which is in September; to an American it is the first of January. This is the first question in my mind. Next, when it's one day here, it's another day somewhere else.

When we speak of a new dispensation, we must understand that it is spiritual and for the Body throughout the entire planet. We cannot base our findings on the American mindset alone. God is listening to and using Messianic Jews and Christians from all over the world. Might I suggest that daybreak comes when time is influenced spiritually? It is as though God's people birth the new season.

The prophets of old prophesied, but in most cases rarely lived to see the prophecy fulfilled. They were told of today, tomorrow, and of the seasons. The people didn't always receive the Word because they didn't see the manifestation immediately. Look at how long Israel waited for her Messiah. In some cases the Lord would say, "when you see this, then this is coming" or "in the fullness of time this will take place."

Influence

There is a release of influence that will establish on earth that which is recorded in Heaven. God can release anyway He desires, but when we think about creation, our purpose, and the road we are to choose, God, whether we like the way it sounds or not, can be highly influenced by us (II Kings 20). This is the way He wants it. He has the power to change the course of the world and to slow down or speed up time. I believe He desires to do it for us as we entreat Him.

Let's look at the word influence: this is a power that can sway the way someone else is thinking, or can change a thought or action. I remember my political days as far back as the mid 1970s. One of the things I learned quickly, and in some cases the hard way, is that people became powerful in this arena by their sphere of influence.

I remember how those with the so-called pull in the higher ranks were respected; when they spoke, everyone listened, and it was amazing to watch. Even when others didn't agree with them, they were able to persuade them to respond as they desired and/or needed.

A person with influence could change the minds of the most powerful leaders, and in turn, affect the entire political strategy with a few words and the right attitude. In fact, if you wanted something done your way, you retained a lobbyist who had the influence to change the minds of the people in high places.

God has a system, a Divine order of events and reasons, and He has agents to carry out His will on earth. When we go to God, as Hezekiah did, we pull on His heart and He responds. His next step is to release His orders into the atmosphere.

Yes, God can do whatever He wants to do, but He wants us to entreat Him and exercise our influence with Him. God, through His grace and a powerful new covenant, gives us influence with Him, which then gives us influence in the heavens.

(Note: This influence is not a deceptive manipulation; God cannot be manipulated. But, God does respond to prayer–and He will change the course of your life for you. This influence is love touching Love; dependence touching Independence; inferior touching Superior.)

Managing the Atmosphere

I recently taught in Colorado Springs on "The Manipulation of the Atmosphere." No one likes the term "manipulation" because it has always been viewed as a cunning evil. Although manipulation can be used for evil, it's really a skillful way to manage, and is, in fact a form of control. To manipulate another human being is not God's way, but what about the atmosphere?

> Wherein in time past ye walked according to the course of this world, according to the prince of the power of the air, the spirit that now worketh in the children of disobedience. (Ephesians 2:2)

There are several important facts concerning the air. First, we must understand that it is a place of release for spiritual things. It is in the air that the Word goes to begin the process of fulfillment. It is the home of light and the home of the dark; the home for sound–words–and the home for silence.

It is also the home for the heavenly hosts and celestial beings. It is in the firmament–the sky right above you–where *satan has his domain. All energy, scientifically and spiritually, comes from this place known as the atmosphere. Scripture tells us that it is divided skillfully to make it a place of habitation for all these things (Genesis 1).

What you are reading is what I've been taught by the *Ruach Ha Kodesh* (His Spirit). It is in the atmosphere where "influence" is released. Whether it be divination, sin, or the Shekinah glory, it is a place for the invisible and the spiritual; and it is here that the supernatural makes its way to you.

Whatever permeates the air around you is going to influence you and the people around you; and whatever the major influence is in the atmosphere will be exactly what you will see manifested. The atmosphere then, is a place of manipulation by either good or evil, dark or light, good spirits or bad spirits.

The Occultic Realm

During the flight between Denver to Colorado Springs, the Lord began speaking to me about the atmosphere. He told me that Colorado Springs was a place that was at war for atmospheric territory/ownership. He allowed me to feel the different pockets in the atmosphere during the flight, in order to prepare me for ministry there. He also told me that although the occultic realm had dominated this atmosphere first and had a very strong divinatory capacity. This capacity was slowly being taken from them by the prophetic ministers He had sent there.

The Lord also showed me that there would be great strategies devised to attempt to bring division in the prophetic camp. Why? Because the prophetic ministers were succeeding in affecting the atmosphere and

* *We do not capitalize "satan" at the risk of grammatical error.*

had become influential in Heaven. I began to see in my spirit the dark at war with the light. The battle over who will govern, control, or skillfully manage the air over Colorado Springs became so vivid to me.

When the occult world rises, it's because the residents there have made what is known as a "capacity" for that influence to reign. When witchcraft or different types of sorcery are released, they can only rule when the "capacity" has been broadened by "influence". Of course, whichever side has the most "*harmony of influence*" will be the dominating influence.

Creating Capacity

By managing the atmosphere over you, you will see either a capacity for good or a capacity for evil. If there is more evil than good it simply means that the Church is not doing its job and the atmosphere is being "influenced" by the dark side. As the people of God, we must create capacity. This is the same concept as occupying (Luke 19:13). Think of the most godly city you have visited and then the most evil. You will quickly see where the influence lies.

The Lord gave us all we need to overcome the darkness. He gave us the reality of creation and His love for us. He sent His only Son to give His Life/Blood for us. That Life/Blood becomes a weapon of authority and war. He released the *Ruach Ha Kodesh* (His Spirit) to inspire us, strategize for us, and promised never to leave us.

When we pray, our words travel straight through the atmosphere like a rocket, piercing the very air we breath. The sound baffles the principalities of darkness and reaches the throne room within a split second. Our words, embraced with love for our God, touch His heart; and He considers our need/request and faith. His love and passion respond.

He Who created and can destroy with a thought, takes our requests and changes everything for you and me. Within another second, He gives His orders to the corporate ladder of heavenly hosts, who then carry out our requests. And now, beloved, you will see the evidence of love; now you obtain a surety that embraces your anointing and ability to take your authority to "influence".

In the eyes of the inhabitants of the air, you now become one of the most influential people they have ever encountered. When there is a harmony—a unity of purpose among God's people on this one petition—angels are with you and devils tremble because they have lost territory and influence. You now obtain control by the hand of God.

The Eyes of God

Daniel 4:13,17 refers to the angels as watchers: "...*behold a watcher and an holy one came down from heaven;" (vs. 13) "...this matter is by the decree of the watchers, and the demand by the word of the holy ones: to the intent that the living may know that the most High ruleth in the kingdom of men..."* (vs. 17). Then, in the Gospel of Luke, we meet Gabriel as the messenger of the Lord. Later, in that same book, we learn that the angels rejoiced at the birth of the Messiah.

We must always keep in mind that the angels are the Hosts appointed by God to carry out His will. They are not to be worshiped or prayed to. In Revelation 19:10 John, the beloved, finds himself in the presence of an angel and falls at his feet to worship him. The angel rebukes him and says to him, "*See thou do it not: I am thy fellow servant, and of thy brethren that have the testimony of Jesus: worship God: for the testimony of Jesus is the spirit of prophecy.*"

To say "fellow servant" is very significant as this speaks of the same obligations toward our God and Messiah. The angel also tells John that he is of his brethren, which refers to the family of creation. All creation is called to serve Him and obey Him. Together they become complete in order to bear the testimony of Jesus Christ. This tells us that only God should be worshiped.

Years ago, when I began teaching on deliverance and spiritual warfare, I found myself too focused on the enemy and his cohorts. I've read many writings on this topic. But, I found most of them focused on the devilish aspect of the heavens, which does exist. However, God, His order, and His Hosts are more powerful. The Lord Yhwh is the Lord of Hosts. This means He influences all Hosts.

Your Army of Support

Generally speaking, the Pentecostal approach to spiritual warfare is to move immediately into yelling and screaming at the devil. Might I suggest that you first influence the heart of God. When you do, He will in turn influence His Hosts of Heaven, who will, in turn, become your army of support.

I can get just as loud as the next person when I get worked up, and I believe when it's done under the anointing it is right. I also believe we have the authority to trample on serpents and scorpions and over all the power of the enemy. I believe nothing will by any means hurt us. However, I must rejoice that my name is written in Heaven (Luke 10:18,19). Why? Because it is in the heavens where the victory begins.

When you, as a child of God, come to your Father and reach into His heart with your need, or as a Church (corporately), you stir the heart of your Bridegroom, His Blood will speak. Influence is then released throughout the heavens, and the earth is affected. Do we have authority? You better believe it. But first, we must influence the heavens. Let's look into the Torah at Exodus 23:20,21:

Behold I send an Angel before thee, to keep thee in the way and to bring thee into the place which I have prepared. Beware of him, and obey his voice, provoke him not for he will not pardon your transgressions: for my name is in him.

There is a great deal pertaining to this Scripture in this writing; however, beware of the angels, because one way or another they will carry out God's plans. They were created to tolerate nothing that gets in the way of God's will. The Lord then says, in verse 22, that if there is obedience to the message sent (the angel's voice) God Himself will be an enemy to his enemies. In other words, I have assigned this angel to carry out My will within My order and to follow My system.

The Holy Spirit is omnipresent; He is always with us and will never forsake us. He is able to make Himself known at any moment, but He also utilizes His angels to carry out His will. That which is beyond human achievement must be accomplished by His Hosts. And, according to Revelation 19:10, we are fellow servants in the testimony of Jesus Christ. This means we are also to carry out His will, within His order, following His system here on earth. We join forces based on heavenly influence.

God has established a structure and that structure is comprised of angels with different jobs and posts. They absolutely will not deviate from God's order unless He changes it. There are overseers—angels who deal with reward and punishment—and angels who deal with the Law of Nature.

These angels only have an ear to God's direction. Praying to an angel makes no sense. Commanding these angels makes no sense, primarily because they are to keep everything the way it has been ordained. When we pray to our Father in Heaven and influence His heart, He will influence the Hosts. Then, His response will be manifested here on earth.

I believe that angels have been active since the beginning of time. I also believe that we are entering a time when we will again see the angelic activity we read about in the Bible. Their activity is going to become more of a reality to us as we enter this new dispensation of time. The more we utilize our influence, the more He will utilize His on our behalf. We will see angels manifest themselves in our services, in hospitals, and in our prayer meetings—not to the glory of the angels, but to the glory of God.

In Zechariah 4:6, the Lord tells Zechariah to tell Zerubbabel that his success in rebuilding the temple is not by might, nor by power, but by His Spirit, and concludes with "*saith the Lord of Hosts.*" In I Samuel 17:45, David spoke to the giant Philistine and said, "*Thou comest to me with a sword, and with a spear and with a shield: but I come to thee in the name of the Lord of Hosts, the God of the armies of Israel whom thou hast defied.*"

The Lord had delivered David from the paw of the lion and out of the paw of the bear (vs. 37). Why was it so important to call Him "Lord of Hosts" at that moment? We learn more in the next chapter. The Lord of Hosts is His name. He does whatever He wants to do at any given time.

He can change what has been ordained in the system on our behalf. Yes, I'm aware that some have had encounters with angels. We've had people testify of seeing angels in our services and on the platform while I'm ministering. I believe there will be a great increase of activity as we enter this time in history. Get ready for the daybreak of the Third Day.

The angels are as the eyes of the Lord running to and fro. Psalm 91:11,12 tells us that He puts angels in charge of us to keep us in all our ways, and to bear us up in their hands. This is only because they are commanded to do so, and they will not leave their post unless their Lord instructs them to.

For the eyes of the Lord are over the righteous, and His ears are open unto their prayers: but the face of the Lord is against them that do evil. (I Peter 3:12)

We never forget that God is the King; He is Almighty and Wondrous. He can accomplish anything by just waving His hand. But, He established His Hosts and created humanity. He sent His only begotten Son to shed His Blood to set us free, and to bring us back to Him. To understand this is to grasp it with the heart, and to realize that you have the ability to change an event. Again, in an attempt to remain balanced, I must say that He can say "no", but He will always live up to His Word.

We are living in the third/fourth watch of the night, which is the early morning before daybreak. I believe this is a time of preparation for the wonderful things that have been prophesied—a time to look within, because Our Lord is about the Father's business.

I believe the Father's mantle has fallen upon many leaders to help rebuild what has been torn down. He will revive the Third Temple, but it shall be built from the inside out. The Spirit of the Lord is crying out for the unity of brotherhood (Ephraim and Israel), and He will hold accountable those who hold back the words given to them by the Lord.

The Harmony of Influence

There is most certainly a dispensational change at the door, but we are not going to see the day break until the influence of God's people partner with the influence of time. God is seeking a *harmony of influence*. Then, He will move on behalf of His loved ones. His angels will become visibly active as they respond to God's direction.

As we influence the heart of God, He will influence His hosts, and they will help us to do His bidding here on earth. The next time you raise your voice in warfare, wouldn't it feel great to know that you have a legion of assigned angels, standing with you? They are His messengers, "the eyes of God".

This is a time when God's people will possess all degrees of favor. I do not speak of periodic moves in a third world country or on a mission trip, but of a time when "Heaven and earth" create a partnership that will shake the planet. Prepare for daybreak. Attach yourself to your Creator.

Divine Favor

Although an entire manuscript could be written on Divine Favor, it is my desire to leave you with the reality of the power of it and to encourage you to study more about it. We know that grace is received freely and not deserved. Favor is different in that a person can have it without deserving it.

However, favor can also be deserved and gained. I'm not speaking of trying to manipulate God, because manipulation is usually devious and for self (temporal) gain. I speak of eternal influence. There are three ways in which I would like to present favor.

- Favor with God (the Lord of Hosts)
- Favor with the angels (the Hosts of God)
- Favor with man

Favor with man is important, because influence is important. But, before you find favor with man, you must find favor with the Lord of Hosts and His Hosts. I must say that I'm sometimes astounded by the favor I feel on my head. When I was a baby in the Lord, I heard people saying to me, "Ask Him for favor." Soon I was asking for it all the time.

Then in 1980, I was invited to President Reagan's Inaugural Ball and all the festivities and private events that went along with it. At the time, I couldn't imagine being able to go because of the high cost of everything. A few days later I received a call from a beautiful couple I had worked with in one of the Congressional races. They wanted to send me to Washington D.C. for all the Presidential festivities. They provided my traveling expenses, my hotel, and all the spending money I needed.

I'll never forget the evening of the Inaugural Ball. I remember sitting in a private box, next to leaders from all over the world. I was very quiet, not understanding why I was there, or what it all meant. I also remember the countless times throughout the years when I walked away from something saying, "Lord, why? What do I do with this?" The Inaugural Ball was one of those times.

To this day, I see favor operating in a magnificent way in my life. I'm not diminishing any favor you have received, I'm just testifying of mine. I'm amazed by some of the things God does for my family and me. This is the favor of God. But, there is more.

When I went to India, I had no idea how I'd be received as a woman. I was not a national figure, but I had a burning message for the Indian people. The men were a little indifferent at first, but within a couple of days they were talking of a mother's anointing on me, asking me to dedicate the land for the work of the Gospel. They crowded the altars during the salvation calls with their families; miracles were taking place—Blessed be His Holy Name!

Favor with Man

I must tell you I felt like a lion that no one could stop. I knew that God was with me. One evening, as I ministered in a Hindu Village, I ran into the street preaching. The pastors ran after me with great concern for my safety, saying, "Sister Irma, the people have seen angels around you. Everywhere you walk they are there. They are visible for everyone to see." I spoke with some of the Pastors who testified of what the people were seeing while I was preaching and I was grateful. But, I was not at all fazed by what I heard, because I was in a supernatural mode.

When I speak of favor with man, I immediately go to the book of Acts (7:10; 24:27; 25:9). Here we see that there is a way to gain favor with man.

> And they were all filled with the Holy Ghost, and began to speak with other tongues, as the Spirit gave them utterance. And there were dwelling at Jerusalem Jews, devout men, out of every nation under heaven. Now when this was noised abroad, the multitude came together, and were confounded, because that every man heard them speak in his own language. And they were all amazed and marvelled, saying one to another, Behold, are not all these which speak Galilaeans? (Acts 2:4-7)

In Acts 2, thousands of souls were converted-at this point, they were all Jews. The disciples of Christ were praising God because they had found favor with all the people, and the Lord kept adding and adding to the Messianic Community. They had found favor with man.

I've noticed that even the most precious people in the Church are not able to receive from you if they have a problem with you. When favor is received from man, they love you and want to hear what you have to say. Whenever I minister in a new Church or foreign land, one of my prayers is for favor with man.

Favor with man is important. God desires to give us favor with man because He desires that we be effective in the building of the Kingdom. There are times when I bring a very hard prophetic word to a church and know I may have become an offense. Yet, I will feel the love and acceptance of the people and the leaders. My goal at that point is to influence on earth as it is in Heaven.

Favor is important because influence is important. The most precious people in the church will not be able to receive ministry if they feel that you have offended them. But, once you receive favor with them, they love you and want to hear what you have to say.

In Luke 1:28 the angel Gabriel appears to Mary saying, *"Hail, thou that art highly favored, the Lord is with thee: Blessed art thou amongst women."* And in verse 30 he says, *"Fear not Mary, for thou hast found favor with God."* Notice how the angel salutes her. *"Hail,"* he says with respect, *"you are highly esteemed in the heavens. You are dignified in our eyes. Fear nothing Mary because you have found favor with God."* When you find favor with God, you become dignified in the eyes of Heaven and are highly respected.

Do Not Pass Me By

In Genesis 18:3, Abraham found favor with God and His hosts. He lifted up his eyes one day and saw three men and ran to meet them and bowed to them. According to the Torah, he looked at the chief one and said, *"If now I have found favor in thy sight, pass not away."* (Don't pass me by; don't let the message pass me by.) Angels are watchers (Daniel 4:13) and they are also Divine messengers.

Abraham says, "Do not pass me by." Soon after that they asked, *"Where is Sarah thy wife?"* (vs. 9) Sarah was in the tent. Then the first message comes forth, *"Sarah, thy wife will have a son"*. (vs. 10) Then, in verse 17, another message comes forth, The Lord says, *"Shall I hide from Abraham what I am about to do?"* He proceeds to prophesy over Abraham and his seed. Then he tells him of the destruction of Sodom and Gomorrah.

First of all, Abraham knew there was a message for him. Secondly, as soon as he receives the message, he begins to exercise his "influence". His influence is more powerful because of the Divine Favor on his head. He now intercedes for Sodom and Gomorrah (vs. 23-33). In the next chapter, we see two angels visiting Lot, and in Genesis 19:13 he receives the message of the coming destruction, which gives him the opportunity to escape.

A Level of Divine Favor

When an individual has Divine Favor in their life, they will find it with God, with the heavens, and with man. This increases their influence tremendously. They become a powerful instrument in every sphere of influence. Divine Favor can be bestowed upon an individual according to their call here on earth. But, there is also a level of Divine Favor that is increased according to the condition of the heart of the individual.

The more we are able to overcome the evil inclination within us, the more Divine Favor we find in everything we do. There is power in the influence we have through Divine Favor. Our power is in invoking the heart of God. Once we have His heart involved, we have increased the magnitude of our effectiveness and all of creation will be moved because of our influence.

Chapter Four

THE HARMONY OF INFLUENCE
Watch and Pray

Have you ever wondered why God had Israel institute prayer at set intervals during the day–the evening sacrifice, midnight, and morning prayers? What about the cycle of the Sabbath? Have you ever considered what would happen if every believer all over the world was praying at the exact same time and asking for the exact same thing? (see Matthew 18:19.)

Many of us wonder why the Jews have a prayer book, and why they all recite the same thing at the same hour with the same understanding. Yes, they even teach the understanding so that they can teach their children to understand with their hearts. This is what brings the power of agreement.

Prayer should not be a repetitive jargon that means nothing to the heart. For Jesus said it is not the many words spoken that reach His heart (see Matthew 6:7). But, learning to set aside specific times of the day for prayer can be very effective. This is why many religions utilize this type of strategy. I call it influence.

Can you imagine getting up at 6:00 a.m. in California when it's 9:00 a.m. in New York and approximately 3:00 p.m. in Israel–knowing that prayers are being released in each of these time zones to invoke the heart of God? Can you imagine being on a mission trip in a remote part of the world–knowing that when you got up to pray during the third/fourth watch of the night that other Christians were on that same clock doing the exact same thing; and that somewhere else in the world it was night time and others were also praying?

> And at midnight Paul and Silas prayed, and sang praises to God: and the prisoners heard them. And suddenly there was a great earthquake, so that the foundations of the prison were shaken: and immediately all the doors were opened, and every one's bands were loosed. (Acts 16:25,26)

Do you really think they were the only ones praying at that moment? And why does the Bible say "at midnight"? It was a watch time. I venture to say that Paul and Silas knew that their brethren were focused on their release as they prayed, sang and praised God during the midnight watch. This was none other than *the power of the harmony of influence*. Probably those at Lydia's house (Acts 16:40) were also praying for them.

The plan is that during the morning watch someone is declaring:

> Hear, O Israel: The LORD our God is one LORD: And thou shalt love the LORD thy God with all thine heart, and with all thy soul, and with all thy might. (Deuteronomy 6:4,5)

Every devoted believer in that time zone is doing the same, while others are at afternoon and evening prayers, in different time zones throughout the world. How powerful it would be if there were a harmony of influence! Why do you think the satanists have midnight times and fasting times together? This is what God intended when He led His people through Israel's leaders to pray at certain strategic times within the same twenty-four hours.

This doesn't mean that He doesn't want you to pray at other times in the day. However, besides your individual efforts, He wants a harmony of influence. Remember, you are powerful in Christ Jesus. This is called "entreating His heart". When you pray, you invoke the heart of God. When many pray at the same time, you establish a harmony of influence that touches God in a way that blesses you and Him.

Evil of the Night

The Bible focuses on the time of the day when important events are recorded. This is why Jesus made it a point to let us know that He prayed at night and worked in the day–that is why there were miracles in His ministry. Nighttime, for example, has a negative association and day-time a positive association. Comments found in Scripture point to a greater authority of wickedness at night (John 9:4; 11:9,10, Romans 13:12, I Thess. 5:5-9).

According to Ephesians 2:2, satan is the prince of the power of the air. He releases a sin energy (temptation) through his cohorts, whose job is to stir the evil inclination of humanity and cause chaos. Although sin is an individual problem which corrupts the social realm, it is supernatural and starts with a release that is almost seductive to the evil inclination of humanity.

Have you ever wondered why more evil takes place at night, or why certain people have devilish dreams at night? Do you ever wonder why believers coming out of the occult are harassed in greater measure at night? Just as the occult centers their focus at a certain interval, Jesus taught us to pray at night.

If you think about it, He went to the temple to pray during assigned intervals, but He also went away alone to pray all night (Luke 6:12). When He did invoke His Father by day it was to teach and on behalf of the people, as when He prayed before raising Lazarus from the dead (John 11:41,42).

Believe it or not, the influence the Lord had at night was instrumental in His day. Think it through carefully: He exercised His influence in Heaven at night and His authority on earth in the day. He had spiritual understanding of the watches of the night. He spoke of watching and praying, of the flesh being weak and the spirit being willing.

In John 9:4 He said, "I must work the works of Him who sent me while it is day." He was our example. He had Divine favor, which caused the earth to shake and graves to open when His purpose was fulfilled. Our influence at night brings us our authority in the day.

There is power in the prophetic hour when you understand the watch within the night or the time within the day. There is power in influence when you overcome evil with good. And there is power in harmony when influence is released in Heaven and on earth.

The Influence of the Illumination of a New Day

At midnight, there is a shifting in things just as there is a rousing up of a new day. I call it the influence of the illumination of a new day–the time in which God releases Divine favor upon His people. This is why the midnight prayer time is said to bring an influence for a renewed day. I speak of prayer and prayer times, and what they accomplish in the different intervals of the day.

> Again I say unto you, that if two of you shall agree on earth as touching anything that they shall ask, it shall be done for them of my Father which is in heaven. For where two or three are gathered in My name there am I in the midst of them.
> (Matthew 18:19,20)

According to Messianic Jewish interpretation, this is actually referring to the Messianic community leaders and their agreement for public order and rules. Jesus promises to support His leaders in their decisions as they are in agreement and alignment with Him. According to Christian interpretation, it refers to prayer. Either way, we are speaking of none other than the harmony of influence.

How do we enter the Third Day? By understanding what time it is! Paul and Silas knew that at midnight the harmony of influence would cause a miracle in that place. We are now in the fourth watch of the Third Day. Daybreak is coming. The more harmony of influence, the greater the impact and the faster the daybreak.

It is not a January first situation in America, although daybreak can come at that moment. It is a call for Divine harmony. There will be no harmony until there is unity. And, there will be no unity until Ephraim and Judah (God's people) become one in His hand (see Ezekiel 37:15).

We are close, even at the threshold, but we must prepare for the harmony of influence. No one knows the exact day and time of any end-time occurrences; no, not even the angels. They stand at their posts day by day, discerning the hour by season not by date and time—ready to carry out all orders from their Creator. Yes, there is a time and date, but it is based on God's fulfillment of prophecy not a human calendar. You will know the "watch" but not in minutes and seconds.

Other than the obvious, I've never fully understood the depth of the effectiveness of proclaimed fasts and congregational prayer meetings. And, I must tell you, that very few of those who call them understand their total effectiveness. But, it is a time to influence Heaven and earth.

God has an order and a system, and His purpose is to cause His will to become action. Sin energy is released supernaturally. It operates on earth like divination to woo the evil inclination within creation (Galatians 5:16-21). According to Scripture, this energy is always active and more effective at night. The power of influence has been given to God's people. It is our covenant right to go to our Father, and because of His love, we have influence.

Jesus knew when it was approaching midnight in the garden. Remember, He came as a man. But, He could have called a legion of angels at any time and they would have listened to Him, because He influenced His surroundings. He had clout in the heavens. He was attached to His Father and He had Divine favor.

The Power of Influence

From the beginning of time, God wanted to be influenced by His creation. He can do whatever He chooses at any time; but, He wants you and I to invoke His heart. In the 1990s, the Church began to focus on unity. Grassroots church communities began to concentrate on building ministerial associations. We heard of the breaking down of the barriers of diversity, and repentance for prejudices; and the Lord began to stir a desire within His people to love each other and work together in harmony. We are on our way to having our spots and wrinkles removed.

He prayed in John 17:21-24, "That they all may be one; as thou, Father, art in me, and I in thee." He also said that we would "be made perfect in one" (vs. 23). This is all part of the fulfillment of Our Lord's prophetic prayer. But what He wants us to understand is that there is power in the influence of harmony.

One of the great strengths of the Jewish people is that although they may have slightly different interpretations within their own camp, they are in agreement with the commandments of the Torah. There are no segregated groups to divide them in the major Biblical issues, only in their level of commitment and social mannerisms.

In their mindset they are all one in Hashem, and they are all taught to believe that they must pray at the appointed times of morning, noon, afternoon, evening, and midnight. Although this is a very individual thing, it is also a very corporate thing, because when they do this they invoke the heart of God as one people and one nation.

Corporate Effectiveness

I'll never forget observing a Jew as he prepared to pray during an international flight. He put on his prayer shawl, faced the East, and quietly recited his morning prayers. I was so blessed to see this type of commitment. As I reflect on it now, I understand what I didn't understand then.

It felt right; it looked right. I now know that it was not only important for him to personally acknowledge God as One, but to also affirm the oneness of Israel in the heavens. "Hear O Israel," (one nation) "The Lord our God is one Lord." The harmony of it brings influence in the heavens. The rest of the Christian Church world finds it very difficult to be corporately effective because of the segregation in Christianity.

To all of you, whether Assemblies of God, Methodist, Baptist, Church of God, Foursquare, etc., I love you all and so does the Lord; but, this is precisely why we have not achieved the harmony of influence on earth. We are fragmented and so self-absorbed. We've learned to parrot the word "unity", but we're not one in our minds. We don't operate as one; therefore, there is no agreement. Although we may have our social differences—and some of us may be more devout than others—we could still have the same foundational mindset of oneness, which brings about an influence of harmony.

If you understand harmony, you understand influence. The more harmony there is, the more powerful your influence. I'm not speaking of a one-world religion, but of a royal priesthood and a holy nation (I Peter 2:9). Isn't it just like our adversary to create a counterfeit for unity such as a one-world religion? A one-world anti-Christ religion would be an oppressive stench upon the earth. You cannot be in agreement with prayers to another god.

The harmony of influence of God's people will be a sweet smelling aroma. If you want power in your personal walk with God, you must obtain influence in the heavens. If you want power in your ministry and in your Church, you must first have a harmony in order to obtain influence. I speak of a harmony of influence that seeks the face of God together before we begin to yell at demons together.

My boldness does not come from the fact that there have been no attempts for pure moves, but rather because the attempts have almost always fallen prey to the enemy's schemes of competition. Competition is a sure way to ruin the harmony of influence. I refer to spiritual matters in the heavens.

Providence

When I think of providence I think of God's influence and His desire to draw all creation to Himself. In Chapter one, I wrote of the root of creation as it pertains to humanity, but He also created the earth—and it is His, and the fullness thereof (Psalm 24). Every detail of creation is completely in His control. He has foreseen all things, knows all things, and has established an order and a system by which to implement His will upon the earth.

We begin our life in darkness with no knowledge of our Creator. In other words, someone must show us the way. From that point on we are as a twenty-four hour span, growing from night to day as we are illuminated with the reality of the great "I Am that I Am." I remember, as a young Catholic girl, sitting in church on Good Friday, weeping at the Stations of the Cross (a service that takes you through each step of the crucifixion).

This was always one of the most enlightening times of the year for me. I was still blind to the Blood of Jesus and why He had to give His life; yet, I could feel the illumination of my Creator coming into my adolescent years. I could feel the "daybreak" of truth bringing more revelation. I always looked forward to this particular service once a year, and fell in love all over again with my Messiah.

It was amazing to me that my Lord would do what He did for me. This is all in God's order and system. As an infant, I was ignorant and in the dark. As a child, I saw in a glass darkly, but began slowly but surely to receive the revelation of God; and some day I'll see Him face to face (I Cor 13:11,12). This is an order and a process that takes me from night to day and from dark to light.

Influence vs. Manipulation

He is God and His fullness is the Father, Son, and Holy Spirit. In His Essence, He can influence anything at anytime. The key to this is that He has planned everything, and has a "future end" for us and for the world; however, He can change whatever He wants to. If He desires to have us influence Him through our prayers, then what is He influenced for? The answer must be this: when we touch Him, He touches Heaven and earth on our behalf-and everything is subject to change.

There are two ways to look at this: first, as a father with a little girl. When I was growing up, I could melt my Daddy's heart. All I really had to do was lock eyes with him and I could influence him. And when I did, I knew He enjoyed it. As a matter of fact, I believe he looked forward to these times because he knew I was going straight for his heart.

The second way to look at this is as a bride with her beloved bridegroom. There is a little jest in men when they speak of the desires of their wives. But the fact of the matter is, when a man cherishes his bride like Christ loves the church (Ephesians 5), she can go to him with the tenderness of her heart, reach into his heart with her helplessness, and he will melt faster than a candle.

She becomes attractive and desirable; and as she reaches for the core of his heart, she will influence him and he will—whether he admits it or not—enjoy it. He becomes her answer. The father and the husband love to become the answer. They long to be the answer. And, the eyes she has for him is the answer that overwhelms him with love.

These two examples should sound very familiar to most of you. As you reach into your Father's heart, you influence (not manipulate) Him. Or, as you go to your husband for a change of plans and reach into his heart, you will influence him. But it doesn't stop there. For once you have influenced God, He now influences everything around Him. And, everything can change, just for you. What a thought! The whole system can change because of you! America can change; your marriage can be saved; and you can be healed!

Here is the entire revelation in a nutshell: If you become an influence in Heaven, earth will be influenced on your behalf. If there is a harmony of influence in the heavens, there will be a harmony of influence here on earth on your behalf. Prepare for daybreak. Understand the Power in the Prophetic Hour. Understand the power in the influence you have as His child, individually, and His Bride corporately.

Chapter Five

THE MANIFESTATION OF THE SONS OF GOD

Revelation Creates Revelation

For I reckon that the sufferings of this present time are not worthy to be compared with the glory which shall be revealed in us. For the earnest expectation of the creature waiteth for the manifestation of the sons of God. (Romans 8:18,19)

The reality of "revelation creating revelation" came alive one summer at a camp meeting at Calvary Temple Worship Center in Modesto, California. There, I had the distinct honor of ministering along side of Dr. Mark Chironna, a man filled with prophetic vision and revelation. It was during that week that the Lord began to speak to me about Romans 8 and the manifestation of the sons of God.

In Isaiah 60:1, the prophet speaks of the glory rising upon us: *"Arise shine; for thy light is come and the glory of the LORD is risen upon thee"*; and again in verse 2: *"The LORD shall rise upon thee, and His glory shall be seen upon thee"*. Then in Matthew 17:2 we read how Jesus was transfigured before them and His face did shine and the glory glowed through His raiment.

In order to paint a verbal picture of the manifestation of the sons of God, I must once again take you to the root of creation that I wrote about in chapter two. The last thing I mentioned within the root of creation was the glory of God, which is to be the ultimate revelation.

The glory of God's image is within us. How do we know this? Because the Godhead, the ultimate revelation, the Word Himself (John1:1) created us. And, revelation creates revelation. We also know that His ultimate purpose in creating us was that we should belong to Him. Revelation must now meet revelation. When creation becomes attached to their Creator, the earthly revelation comes face to face with heavenly revelation.

The Glory of Earthly Revelation

Where did this glory come from? The root of creation! It is the glory of earthly revelation, the manifestation of the sons of God. When Jesus took His disciples up to the mount of transfiguration, "His Body" shone with the glory. Who's Body? His Body!

Prophetic revelation was set forth visually for His disciples. His Body is the Church—you and I—the sons of God. His Body houses His glory. This glory, at the fullness of times, would rise upon His Body and it would show Itself.

We begin by *yada* (Hebrew for knowing the revelation) and then finally we *ra'ah* (Hebrew for seeing the revelation). If revelation is invisible, we must obtain an ability to see with prophetic vision. And finally, He manifests the reality of it by *ni'rah* (Hebrew for showing Himself). Remember also that during the fourth watch, He showed Himself willingly as they awaited daybreak. I repeat: within your root is a good and evil inclination, promises yet to be fulfilled, His image, and His glory. The glory of His creation.

In Genesis 1:26 we read, *"God said, Let US make man in our image, after our likeness..."* The word "US" has stirred within the Church for years. The fact of the matter is that "US" was indeed truly Elohim, the One True God. "US" was Elohim, with all of His Essence, which includes all of Who He is: Father, Son and Holy Ghost (all in One); His character, His nature, His love, His mercy, His grace, His wisdom—and on and on. At that very moment in time, all His Hosts were also present. The ultimate Revelation created revelation.

Revelation is the dramatic disclosure of something not formerly known or realized. Revelation will actually manifest the hidden. And, something that is revelatory contains things not realized and out of the normative.

If God, Who surpasses all boundaries of the normative, Who houses things that surpass our human natural understanding, has created us, He has brought forth the revelation that houses the "hiddeness" of His image. This means that Revelation has created revelation, which can only bring more revelation.

I'm convinced that, just as God cannot lie, He cannot create something that is not revelation. Everything brought forth and breathed upon by Him must have the capacity to house the extraordinary. All creation is groaning for the dramatic manifestation of His Divine Truth and Essence.

The Metaphor of Travail

> For we know that the whole creation groaneth and travaileth in pain together until now. (Romans 8:22)

Isn't it curious that the inspired Word of God uses the metaphors of birth pangs and travail in the illustrating of spiritual manifestations? How does a man travail? How does the whole creation groan with travail, and why?

The first thing we must realize is that one of the most mysterious metaphors in the Bible seems to be that of humanity becoming a female in the eyes of God. In Song of Solomon, we see the depiction of the bridegroom and the bride as God and Israel. In Ephesians 5:32, the mystery refers to Christ and the Church.

Obviously, we as the female in the union, were created to procreate. This makes me realize how awesome it is to be a woman. And, it helps me better understand the deeper truths in this metaphor. As a woman, I feel so protected and supernaturally provided for. It is also just as awesome to be a man, as there is a deeper understanding of the feeling our Lord must have toward His daughter and His bride. Man of God, how loved you must feel by your Creator!

The metaphor of travail makes sense now:

> For we know that the whole creation groaneth and travaileth in
> pain together until now, and not only they, but ourselves also,
> which have the first fruits of the Spirit, even we ourselves groan
> within ourselves, waiting for the adoption, to wit, the redemp-
> tion of our body. (Romans 8:22,23)

All creation is in travail! The righteous and the sinner groan inside
to see the hidden truth of creation as they pant for *yada* (to know) and
ra'ah (to see) and *ni'rah* (for Him to show Himself). This will surface at the
manifestation of the sons of God. The sinner travails in sin while the
righteous travail in prayer and function. There is no middle ground. This
means you are doing one or the other.

What is Being Pushed Through the Birth Canal?

Remember, the Jewish perspective of interpretation. It is said that
all of humanity has an evil inclination as well as a good inclination.
Otherwise, we would have no free will and no choices to make. And, from
the Genesis of time, God wanted us to make a choice.

Within the birth canal is the substance of the root of creation and
all that it contains. We carry a child in the womb for its term, and at the
fullness of time, the child enters the birth canal and there is a pushing and
groaning until that which has been carried is birthed. There is a struggle,
because that which is within must now come out and show itself to the
world.

We as the Church, have been carrying the substance of revelation—the prophetic promises and destiny of the Church, the image of God
(not the image of man or the world), and to which is the glory of God.
We are His revelation surfacing for the fullness of times. The sinner, the
lost, and all of creation groans and pushes in preparation for the manifestation of the sons of God, the revelation of His glory, and the glory of all
creation.

The Spirit of Prophecy has joined in the travail. He has become our coach in the labor room. He grieves for creation. He knows what He created and what His intent was before man trampled on it with "choice".

The harlots and the drug dealers are in travail because they want to see what they house come forth. They don't know they are in travail. But, every time they act out within their lifestyle, they are crying out for a birthing for "their original intent". They might even visit a church to see if they can "see" love and hear some "good news". But, unfortunately, most will find only judgment, condemnation and excommunication.

You see, the nature of Jesus is hidden within us and we won't let Him out. We have Him covered up with denominational theology, and self-absorbed opinions that cause the sinner to run back to the streets. The Spirit of the Lord is pulling on us to repent for our ignorant foolishness.

I'm convinced that all the prostitute wants is a mother's love and guidance. I'm persuaded that the sinner living in a lying world only wants to know if there is such a thing as truth. My visits to the men's prison in northern California have taught me well.

When they come under the influence of the love of God, they begin to see that there is hope for what is truly inside of them and inside others. They can't put it into words, but they know *(yada)* which makes them a candidate for *ra'ah* (seeing with the inner eye) and then finally the Lord will bring *ni'rah* (the revelation). The mission is to birth His glory, which will manifest throughout His creation.

Chapter 6

THE SPIRITUAL ECLIPSE OF THE HOUR

The Power Encounter Has Begun

In 1999, the Lord spoke to me about a coming Spiritual Eclipse that would cover the earth. He took me to Isaiah, where the prophet says:

> Arise, shine; for thy light is come, and the glory of the LORD is risen upon thee. For, behold, the darkness shall cover the earth, and gross darkness the people: but the LORD shall arise upon thee, and his glory shall be seen upon thee. (Isaiah 60:1,2)

Most of the time, when the Lord speaks to us about something of this magnitude, we don't grasp it's full meaning immediately. In other words, everything unfolds and unveils itself in His time. Some things may appear within days or months. But, because God works through progressive process, in most cases it will be a matter of years before we see them fulfilled.

In order to focus on the message as a metaphor for something God wanted to convey to me, and to His Church, I had to first learn about the nature of an Eclipse. I also found several references in the Holy Scriptures having to do with this phenomenon:

> The earth shall quake before them; the heavens shall tremble: the sun and the moon shall be dark, and the stars shall withdraw their shining. (Joel 2:10)

> The sun shall be turned into darkness, and the moon into blood, before the great and the terrible day of the LORD come. (Joel 2:31)

> And I will shew wonders in heaven above, and signs in the earth beneath; blood, and fire and vapour of smoke: The sun shall be turned into darkness, and the moon into blood, before that great and notable day of the Lord come. (Acts 2:19,20)

> And God said, Let there be lights in the firmament of the heaven to divide the day from the night; and let them be for signs, and for seasons, and for days, and years. (Gen 1:14)

The phenomena of an Eclipse–whether solar or lunar–is that it always includes light and darkness. An eclipse always brings together that which is heavenly and earthly for a moment in time. It is almost as if there is a battle between the two to pierce and cover one another. As one overtakes the other, there is a red highlight, which seems to show itself like blood.

Some saw an Eclipse as an omen of the judgment to come. The Hebrew prophets saw it as a sign of God's power and authority. They knew the hand of their God and would not be alarmed.

> Thus saith the LORD, Learn not the way of the heathen, and be not dismayed at the signs of heaven; for the heathen are dismayed at them. (Jeremiah 10:2)

The Signs of the Times

Some might think it superfluous to ponder the signs of the times. However, Jesus, Himself, when confronted by the Pharisees and Sadducees about showing them a sign, responded first by explaining that there is a difference between discerning by the common uniform signs of the weather and the spiritual eye (see Matthew 16:1-4).

David Stern, author of The Jewish New Testament Commentary, says there are three ways to discern:

1. The appearance (face) of the sky, which merely foretells the natural weather.

2. A sign from God.

3. The signs of the times, which evoke both weather, seasons, and where we stand in the flow of history.

History is a natural progression, which is directly linked to the progression of the heavens and all their Hosts. The "progressive process" of the fulfillment of God's plan, which could be said to be a fourth method of discernment, speaks of this link and the ability to recognize its thread in what is happening today.

Jesus knew that those He was addressing saw by the natural, misleading predictions of the astrologers and monthly prognosticators (see Isaiah 47:13). Those who arrived at conclusions without discerning by the Spirit of God were, in Jesus' opinion, a wicked and adulterous people-wicked, because they were always questioning and doubting Him in their hearts; adulterous, because they sought their answers through other mediums.

When the Pharisees and the Sadducees asked Jesus for a sign from Heaven, He called them hypocrites because they could discern the face of the sky, but could not discern "the signs of the times". (See Matthew 16:3.) He refused to give a sign to those who questioned Him, because the intent of their heart was wicked and adulterous (see vs. 4).

I know at that moment, in His heart, He must have been thinking: You have overlooked the greatest of signs in your quest for more. The Kingdom of God has come upon you, and you do not even know it! This was the day of their visitation, but they were oblivious to the presence of the Messiah.

There are many intelligent and well-educated people throughout the world today who are not seizing this moment in time. It matters not when you read this, there are moments for you to seize. This was a moment in time for them and they could not see with the eye of the Spirit.

Our Lord showed them many signs and miracles. His very Words penetrated their hearts. Yet, they sought after more in order to prove that He was not Who He said He was. Nowhere in the Holy Scriptures does it say that signs are evil. Neither is it wrong to get in the flow of the signs of the times. It is wrong to ask for more when the signs are already there.

There is a process that brings about the fulfillment of things:

1. The Lord has to give the orders.

2. The heavenly Hosts must get involved and carry them out.

3. It must fit into the natural flow of history, which seems to begin in Israel.

4. The eye of the spirit of mankind must begin to stir.

5. The natural turns into a metaphor for the spiritual and there is a manifestation of the two.

Prophets and ministers have preached under the prophetic anointing about Heaven and earth kissing. This, to me, is the incredible link, which brings "The Prophetic Power of the Hour."

The Prophetic Power of the Hour

A few days after I released the message on the Eclipse to a Church in California, I received a call from the Pastor telling me there was going to be an actual Eclipse in Israel within the next few days. The pastor said that the Eclipse would cover the Middle East. At that time–the summer of

1999–I knew nothing more except that the Lord was affirming my message within the natural scope of things.

I believe that at the time of this writing we are seeing the beginning of the reality of a Spiritual Eclipse–a struggle between light and dark. Israel has undergone horrific terror for years from those who hate them. They have fought the good fight of faith as terrorists plot against their lives and economy.

On September 11, 2001, this poison made its way to America as terrorists hijacked four of our commercial jetliners. Two of them headed to New York's lower Manhattan area to destroy the World Trade Center, an edifice that represented the nations of the world.

Minutes later, another jetliner made its way to Washington, D.C. and crashed into the Pentagon, which represents the mind of America and the master intelligence of the world. A fourth jetliner aimed at The White House, symbolic of the head of our country and one of the superpowers of the world, went down in Pennsylvania. I believe this to be a sign of the times. We need not ask for more!

These events are as a "Spiritual Eclipse" whereby the Kingdom of Darkness and the Kingdom of God have merged in a battle. Darkness (in the form of terrorism) figuratively covered the earth as it penetrated the World Trade Center-and gross darkness as thousands lost their lives. The evident talk of war has now made its way into our remedy. All the while, I knew deep in my heart that this same war was also in full force in the heavens.

In all this, there is one thing we must never forget regardless of the time in history in which you read this book: when there is war on earth–there must be war in Heaven. There must be victory in the spiritual realm before there is victory on earth.

The End-Time Army

At this moment in time, there is a parallel battle from which the Holy Community (the Body of Christ) cannot deny or run from. We are joining as fellow servants with His heavenly hosts here on earth. The Spirit of the Lord is now fulfilling the prophetic words that have been released for years: "God is raising up an End-Time Army".

This Army will fight the battle in the Spirit like faithful soldiers go to war in the natural. The Church will lose sleep to prayer like soldiers in the natural war lose sleep for survival. They will fast and purposely miss meals like soldiers in this natural war miss meals in the midst of battle.

This Spiritual Army (the Church) will have a *kavana* (Hebrew for "aim") that will bring discernment and accuracy in the Spirit. This Army, called by some as "this generation", has nothing to do with age. It will be comprised of people of all ages (75 year olds and 15 year olds) who are living in this privileged time in history. Jesus, spoke of the signs preceding the advent of His second coming:

> And there shall be signs in the sun, and in the moon, and in the stars; and upon the earth distress of nations, with perplexity; the sea and the waves roaring; men's hearts failing them for fear, and for looking after those things which are coming on the earth; for the powers of heaven shall be shaken. (Luke 21:25,26).

Then in verse 28, He said, *"And when these things begin to come to pass, then look up, and lift up your heads; for your redemption draweth nigh"*. This is advice worth following when we see the signs of the times unfolding.

Our Lord told the prophet Isaiah that darkness would surely cover the earth and gross darkness the people. He told Joel that the earth would quake and a redness like blood would cover the earth; but he also said, "the LORD shall arise upon thee, and his glory shall be seen upon thee." This means, all that is within His people, the root of creation–His Image, His promises, and His nature–is going to rise above the battle, above the rubble, and above the darkness.

He said the gentiles, which is really to say "the nations", would be drawn to the light–glory seen on us. (See Isaiah 60:3.) In the midst of the Eclipse, we will become a bright light that will draw all men unto Him. Blessed be His Holy Name! It is the manifestation of the Sons of God.

The Wings of the Morning–Daybreak is Coming

Psalm 139:9-12 declares, *"If I take the wings of the morning, and dwell in the uttermost parts of the sea; Even there shall thy hand lead me, and thy right hand shall hold me. If I say, Surely the darkness shall cover me; even the night shall be light about me. Yea, the darkness hideth not from thee; but the night shineth as the day: the darkness and the light are both alike to thee".* And, in Malachi 4:2,3 we read, *"But unto you that fear my name shall the Sun of righteousness arise with healing in his wings; and ye shall go forth, and grow up as calves of the stall. And ye shall tread down the wicked; for they shall be ashes under the soles of your feet in the day that I shall do this, saith the LORD of hosts."*

It might look grossly dark for a moment. The light may seem to have disappeared, but suddenly a bright light will break through the darkness as the morning of a new day. It is said that this light is as a crown with wings (called the wings of the morning) that Malachi spoke of. The light of His glory and His creation cannot be snuffed out and it cannot be covered.

Do not be moved by the "Spiritual Eclipse of the hour". The King of the Universe–the One True God–He, and He alone, has a plan and He cannot be stopped. He will turn all things that the kingdom of darkness attempted to overtake to naught. If you love Him…if you serve Him…if you stand before Him in covenant…you will manifest His glory as it rises upon you. Daybreak is coming!

United We Stand!

Something happened to America through this catastrophe. Now, all that seemed so fragmented between Democrats and Republicans, Baptist and Pentecostals, has changed. When the people in those hijacked jetliners looked at each other for the last time, they were not looking at skin color or economic status. When the people running down the stairs of the World Trade Center in New York knew they wouldn't make it, nothing mattered except life itself.

When the loved ones waited on the street for news about their sister, brother, spouse, son or daughter, it no longer mattered who was white collar and who was blue collar, who was president, vice president or mail clerk. The reality settled in. We are not complete without each other. We only become whole with each other.

A census was taken in the nation of Israel during Old Testament times. Some might think it was for the purpose of counting heads. However, there was a powerful message in this as each life was to be counted with a half of a shekel. You see, they were whole pieces that were not complete unless they came together as a united (Holy) nation. The counting of heads was forbidden because there is only One Head over Israel, and that is the One True God (see Exodus 38:26; Numbers 1; II Samuel 24:1-9; I Chronicles 21:1-8). Without the unity of a nation (a people) there will be no harmony. The sound will not reflect the Head.

God will bring us to a place of unity where I am willing to stand with you and you with me. Not only must creation become whole, but the harmony of the sound we make must become whole. I need you and you need me. When it is all said and done, nothing else matters except Our Creator and His intent for us. We must stand together to see the glory of the Lord rise upon us. This is the Image of God!

Between the Seeds–The Image of God

In Genesis 1:27,28 according to the traditional Hebrew text, we read, *"And God created man in His image, in the image of God He created Him; male and female He created them. God Blessed them and God said to them, be fertile and increase, fill the earth and master it; and rule the fish of the sea, the birds of the sky, and all the living things that creep on earth."* The King James version uses the words, "replenish, subdue, have dominion".

What is it that He was really saying? The soul of mankind is the wonder of the Lord. If He made us in His Image, then mankind has a place of honor here on earth and we are supposed to highly esteem the sanctity of life. If He made us in His Image and there was no procreation, then the Image of God would become obsolete. What He is really saying, is "MULTIPLY MY IMAGE over and over on earth, from generation to generation."

It is no wonder, then, that the battle is between seeds. Genesis 3:15 (traditional Hebrew text) reads, *"I will put enmity between you and the woman and between your offspring and hers; they shall strike at your head and you shall strike at their heel".* The Lord cursed the serpent and told him that on his belly he would crawl and eat dirt. This meant that there would be an ongoing battle between these:

1. The seed of woman.

2. The Messiah and redeemed mankind.

3. The serpent and unredeemed mankind.

It is clear by His Words that the serpent can go no higher than the heel, because he cannot not reach any higher. It is further clear that the Messiah and redeemed mankind will bring a deadly blow to the serpent's head. You will also remember, that because we have dominion over every kind of animal, we have dominion over him.

I remind you that our battle is not with flesh and blood. The battle is in the spiritual realm because this is where we win or lose. The battle is between the forces of God and the forces of the serpent. The seed of woman will bring a deadly blow to the head of the serpent. And, the seed of the serpent will strike at our heel, because he cannot reach any higher.

The battle is about the Image of God. The battle is about precious souls.

The Image of God–Your Weapon of Spiritual Warfare

Within you (the root of creation) is the Image of God. The stronger you get, the more the Image of God is going to shine through. This, in turn, brings His glory. God has no similitude. He is Spirit! Therefore, the Image and measure of His Spirit that He has placed in us must make its debut (Isaiah 60:1).

This very Image is what will pierce the gross darkness of this Eclipse that I am speaking of. If you are weak in the Spirit–if you are anemic in your communication with your Creator–you will miss your full purpose in life. The Image of God is in your soul, beloved. And, He, in His Grace, is pulling on your heart to take heed to the voice of the Prophets.

If you are a part of the Body of Christ (redeemed), you have been marked for the Battle of the Lord–and He is the Captain of His Hosts. The Image of God shall rise upon you and you will pierce the darkness.

"To Him who has ears to hear, let him hear".

Sing Unto the Lord a New Song

When I think of the word sing, I think of music, voices, and harmony. When I think of the word new, I think of something having been discovered and coming to the surface. I've heard it said that there is no new revelation. Truly, when talking about the Word of God in terms of adding or deleting to the Word, I agree. However, this book may have given you new revelation. It may have brought to the surface something you had not discovered before.

I'd like to take a moment to look at the word sing–not from a theological sense, but from a practical and figurative sense. To sing is to utter sounds in musical tones. It is to make a proclamation from the depth of your being. In order to release the sound of this proclamation, there must be something that resonates within.

I've never been a singer, yet something resonates within me. When I'm on the platform in the middle of ministry, I can hear a sound resonating within me. The anointing motivates the release of it and brings either an introduction to the next move of God and/or the actual move of God. When that happens, it is new and fresh.

In Psalm 96:1,2 we read, *"O sing unto the LORD a new song: sing unto the LORD, all the earth. Sing unto the LORD, bless his name; shew forth his salvation from day to day."* This *Shir-Chadash* (Hebrew for "New Song") is precipitated by a universal call to all humanity to come together with a new sound–a union of all humanity in a praise of their Creator. It is a phenomenon motivated by revelation and anointing, which has been developing with time, through the ages, to bring renewal and regeneration (revival).

Birthing the New Song

When you sing prophetically, you sing in the present tense, in contemplation of the future. When you sing this New Song, it will be due to the discoveries (apocalyptic, unveiling of His Essence) about our God, our Creator. The prophetic song is based on insight. The insight ends up in the unveiling of Who He is in the matter. This, in turn leads to birthing the New Song.

To sing the Word of God will stir your innermost being and prepare you for *Shir-Chadash*. Uttering the sound that God is giving you for the moment, in word or musical tones, contemplates the future and takes you to new discoveries in Him.

Those that do not believe that the Divine Inspiration of the Spirit of Prophecy is alive and intense today, will not agree with me. As a worship leader and/or worshippers, you may know you've hit a wall. You've taken the people as far as you can with what you're doing. However, deep down inside you know there is more—much more.

God is wanting to give you *Shir-Chadash* (a New Song). This song is not necessarily a song like we know it. It is a way of life. The New Song is a sound that resonates from a discovery deep inside of us. It will take you and those you lead to new heights and discoveries. God wants to take you higher and higher, closer and closer.

Throughout this book, the possibility of harmony is presented to the reader as a partner to power and co-laborer to apocalyptic (unveiling) times. I would like to suggest to you that this *Shir-Chadash* (New Song) is going to be the harmony of creation celebrating their Creator and His creation. All Creation will sing a New Song unto the Lord.

The more revelation we receive, the closer we come to making a harmonious sound that will join us together with our fellow servants in Heaven. The more in harmony we become, the more spiritually influential we will become. The Divine Inspiration we have felt for the hidden manna in the last few years has brought great discoveries for the Body of Christ.

The discoveries of His greatness, His love, His power, and His Blood have caused the new sound to resonate within you. This is a song that no man can stop and no devil can quiet down. We are approaching the call for the universal *Shir-Chadash* (New Song). What we are experiencing now is a preparation, which is causing a rehearsal within the Holy Community. This is *The Prophetic Power of the Hour.* LET THE SONG BEGIN!

Experience the Fountain of Fatherhood

The day and the hour has come for the mantle of The Father, *Abba,* to come upon the Body of Christ. The Lord spoke this word from His Heart to me to share with you:

"For there are many that have not felt the love of a father, and others call on one, but have never experienced one. This has created a schism between us. My sorrow is multiplied because you will not come close to Me and you will not "experience Me".

You cannot know Me unless you "experience Me". You cannot "experience Me" unless you draw close to Me and touch My heart. I am more than your Creator, I am your Abba, Father. I am He who thought you through before you were manifested into a reality. An earthly father does not know what kind of seed shall come forth; he is fruitful and trusts in nature. But your Heavenly Father–He thinks through what He does before He does it. I saw your today, yesterday, and I have planned your tomorrows in My heart.

If you think you were not planned—if you think you are not ade-
quate—if you think you cannot serve Me with a whole heart . . . think again,
my beloved—for I have thought you through and brought you to a place
where you will be challenged in your very soul to "experience Me".
Because of your earthly experience, you have become spiritually handi-
capped. My heart has become a wilderness to you—and you have not wanted to draw close. Do not fear Me as you would an earthly father. Do you
not know that which you see is not with the inner eye of experience? For
in My heart there is a Fountain for you that springs forth the fulfillment of
all you ever needed. Out of this Fountain comes the Author of
Fatherhood. All you could ever need is within My heart and it will spring
forth forcefully on your behalf.

There is a Fountain for you in My heart. Until you experience this
Fountain, you will not truly know Me. Draw close to Me, my beloved, I
am your Abba, Father. I have created you and how I long to Father you!
Reach for My heart. Do not be afraid to "experience Me". I will make the
mountain you face a plain for you. I will root up that which has torment-
ed you. I will raise up a standard on your behalf. Take your heart off of
carnal highs and your eyes off of gain—and look to Me. Draw close, I AM
HE—YOUR LOVING, ABBA, HOLY, RIGHTEOUS, FAITHFUL,
AND LOYAL FATHER. COME TO ME AND EXPERIENCE THE
FOUNTAIN OF FATHERHOOD. REACH FOR MY HEART—AND
YOU WILL EXPERIENCE WHO I AM."

Footnote: Eternal life is not limited to heaven. The Hebrew thought
behind eternal life is founded on experiencing what has been revealed.
Whatever He is as you know Him must be experienced. *"And this is life eternal, that they might know thee the only true God, and Jesus Christ, whom thou has
sent."* (John 17:3)

EPILOGUE

AMERICA STRIKES BACK

I find it spiritually provoking that at the time of this writing America is at war. This is an unusual war in that it is, I believe, the first time that America has been involved with what some are calling a "Holy War". This is an implication that recruits culture, religion, government, politics, economy, and all civilians. It means that all of the components of all that we stand for as a nation are threatened in one way or another.

The war has erupted in Afghanistan and is clearly not against the Afghan people. The war is waging against a group that call themselves the Taliban and one of their heroes Osama bin Laden. These people are said to be the perpetrators of the most tragic attacks on America since Pearl Harbor in 1941. There is another aspect to this battle that has been in a state of denial for years: "Terrorism".

This begins with the battle of the mind, plainly called "Psychological Warfare". The enemy works on penetrating the mind of the opponent with terror, introducing thoughts of the sting of death through horrific acts like biological warfare and nuclear mass destruction. The psychology of it is that you are not sure what is hype or bluff and what is not.

We are supposed to wonder when our aircraft will be hijacked or when a facility we are in will be blown up or infested with Anthrax. This inevitably is to effect the economy as normal lifestyles come to a halt. We are supposed to fear what we eat and drink and get in the mail. All of this while spending all our free time watching the news, terrified for our families. This enemy is not afraid to die and will sacrifice their life for their cause. They are capable of suicide in order to brutally kill many at one time.

The Parallel Battle

There is a parallel battle that is being fought in the heavens. It is a power encounter that has recruited redeemed mankind. Those that know the One True God, who have been given spiritual authority by the Blood of Jesus Christ are slowly but surely answering the call. This is truly a Holy War.

Our opponent has one captain and we have another. His name is "I Am". His name is "The Lord of Hosts". His name is "Faithful and True". Elijah, when dealing with Ahab, Jezebel, and the false prophets said: "The God that answers with fire, let Him be God". In this hour we will see "God be God!"

What our opponent does not realize is that God did not give us a spirit of fear, but of power, love and a sound mind (see II Timothy 1:7). Through Jesus Christ, *death has been swallowed up in victory*, and the only sting of death is through sin. (see I Corinthians 15:54)

If you know Him, you cannot help but be persuaded that neither death nor life, nor angels, nor principalities, nor power, nor things present, nor things to come, nor height, nor depth, nor any other creature, shall be able to separate us from the love of God, which is in Christ Jesus Our Lord. (Romans 8:38,39)

He said the following signs would follow them that believe: in His Name you will cast out devils, you will speak with new tongues, you will take up serpents, and if you drink anything deadly it shall not hurt you. And, on top of all that you will lay hands on the sick and they will recover". (Mark 16:17,18)

Nothing is more powerful than the Blood of Jesus Christ. What we must not ever forget is that we overcome by that very Blood and we, too, love not our lives unto death!

Regardless of the generation that reads this or what the date is, never forget that God is a faithful God and is a God that keeps covenant. Believe in Him and stand on His Word and you will always see results. Do not fear the venom of the enemy, for the Lord Our God, HE IS GOD and there is no other.

–Irma Elizabeth Diaz

MINISTRY VISION

"To Attach Creation to Their Creator." ™

OTHER PRODUCTS AVAILABLE

The Breath of God *by Irma Elizabeth Diaz*

The Breath of God *(Ruach Ha Kodesh)* is charging the spiritual atmosphere, making it pregnant with the anticipation of God's plan for our generation.

This powerful, wonderful Breath of God is increasing the challenge to God's people to step out into the purposes of God with faith and courage. But, the Bride of Christ must first put away selfish pursuits and fleshly ambitions.

She must open herself to receive that Holy Breath. Irma Elizabeth Diaz has skillfully drawn a "treasure map" for God's people who are hungry and willing to dig for the treasure God has already deposited within them. *The Breath of God* is a must-read for any serious Christian who longs for the heavenly consummation of the greatest union of all time. ISBN 0-7684-3025-9 Paperback 126 pages

For More Information or Products

This book as well as a variety of Rev. Irma's preaching and teaching audio cassettes and series are available for purchase using VISA or MasterCard.

Please call Upon This Rock Ministries toll-free at (888) 567-7474 to purchase or for a listing of topics and titles.

HOW TO CONTACT US

UPON THIS ROCK MINISTRIES
Post Office Box 2146
Covina, California 91722
USA

(888) 567-7474

WWW.IRMADIAZ.ORG